Fifth Dimensional Healing

Remove Physical, Mental, Emotional
and Spiritual Blockages
and Claim your Divine Sovereignty

by

Christina Martine

The information contained within this book is not designed to cure, heal or replace professional medical advice from your medical practitioner. The contents of this book are to be used as a guide to assist you in making important choices that will help you lead a more healthy, peaceful and blissful life. The author does not prescribe any of the materials or techniques presented in this book as a treatment for any illness or medical condition. Consult with your medical practitioner before changing your diet and health regime.

Cover Design by Dusan Arsenic

Interior design by ipublicidades.com

Edited by Barbara Lauger

ISBN: 978-1-7752409-0-7

Acknowledgements

Thank you, Charlotte Brown, for editing my first draft
and for being a constant source of inspiration and love.
Thanks to my partner, Erik Brommell, for your unending love
and for listening to my theories. Thank you, my guides,
angels and countless mentors, for without your support
this book could not have been written.
Lastly, thank you, God, for this beautiful existence
and opportunity to be.

Contents

Glossary

5D Redo: A Fifth Dimensional Healing technique that enables you to heal and transmute painful memories and traumas from your past.

5th Dimension: The fifth dimension is a vibrational aspect of consciousness that enables souls to move freely through time and space in a non-linear fashion.

5th Dimensional Healing: A holistic healing method channelled to Christina Martine from the fifth dimension, which incorporates energy healing, visualization, channelling and magical intention. The techniques are:

- It's Safe to Feel
- Seven Golden Orbs of Light
- 5D Redo
- 5D Healing Technique to Heal the Liver
- 5D Healing Technique to Heal the Spleen
- 5D Healing Technique to Heal the Lungs
- 5D Healing Technique to Heal the Kidneys
- 5D Healing Technique to Heal the Heart
- Energetic Organ Cleanse
- Chakra Cleanse

Anti-nutrients: Detrimental substances found in grains that are toxic to the human body. Lectin, phytic acid and gluten are examples.

Akashic Records: Knowledge within the seventh density oversoul where all thoughts, emotions, sensations and memories from all lifetimes are recorded for all of eternity.

Angel: Spirits whose main mission is to heal. Some angels have previously had human lives and others have never been incarnate. As a human, currently you have already been in angelic form, moving from a higher density into the lower one here on Earth. You will once again return to your angelic state of consciousness as you remember who you are.

Animal Guide: A spirit guide in animal form that helps you align with your soul.

Arcturians: Fifth dimensional star beings from the Boötes constellation. One of the oldest races in the universe, they are master healers, scientists and inventors who understand that we are truly all one.

Astrology: An ancient art form and divination tool that uses the position of the stars to help you discover more about the journey of your soul. Knowing what's going on within the stars is like getting an energetic forecast that tells you when it's a beneficial time to make certain choices with your free will.

Being: The soul or true self.

Chakras: The root, sacral, solar plexus, heart, throat, third eye and crown make up the seven main chakras, or energy centres, in your body. Chakras that are cleared enable you to channel subtle energy to keep you healthy and strong.

Channelling: A spiritual practice where you receive information through your psychic channels. This may come in the form of writing, speaking, art, music, etc.

Demon: Entities that have strayed off their true soul path to explore their own darkness. Demons exist below the first density of consciousness, in the underworld. Demons can be created as thoughtform entities through magical intention as well.

Density: Densities are areas of consciousness that you move into from Source. To visualize the densities, imagine life is a video game simulation. Every density that gets created from Source, all the way down to the first, is like a level you have to play through. We move from Source down to the first density to start the game. Then we move up through the densities back up to Source to win the prize of eternal life with no suffering.

Dimension: Dimensions are the characteristics of the densities, or video game levels, of consciousness. Dimensions determine what the beings look like in each density and how they will respond to their environment. The first three densities are fourth dimensional, where time and space are linear and difficult to manipulate. The fourth, fifth and sixth densities are fifth dimensional, where time and space are non-linear and much easier to manipulate. The seventh density and beyond is non-material and timeless.

Dis-ease: Dis-ease is disharmony that occurs within the body. All dis-ease comes from a spiritual blockage first. When you heal the soul, the mind and body follow.

Divine Being: A sacred being of Source. We are all divine beings.

Divine Channel: Someone who has their psychic channels open and has the ability to channel spiritual information or messages.

Divine Consciousness: Awareness in alignment with the creator.

Divine Expression: An honest sharing of speech, emotion, movement, etc., that comes directly from your heart, in alignment with the creator. Divine expressions are healing for the world and align you with your true soul path.

Elf: An earth spirit that usually can be found in the forest.

Empath: Someone who can feel the emotions of others.

Fairy: An air spirit that can usually be found in flower gardens.

Gnome: An earth spirit that can usually be found in forests.

Higher self: A version of you that exists in a higher density, usually in the fifth or sixth. Your higher self is fifth dimensional and has more power to manifest than you currently do. You can call upon your higher self for guidance at any time, as it's never separate from you.

Initial Soul Detour: An initial soul detour is the point when you first make the choice to stray away from the path your soul wants you to take.

Kun Gong: The kun gong (pronounced kwun gawng) is a sacred energy centre located behind the navel that produces yuan jing (pronounced ywen jing), yuan qi (pronounced ywen chee) and yuan shen (pronounced ywen shun). Yuan means original, so yuan jing, yuan qi, and yuan shen are original jing, original qi and original shen.

Light Body: Your non-material, astral body that you use to travel back to Source each night. Upon death, you will retain this body and use it to travel to higher densities and dimensions.

One Consciousness: Source consciousness, where all is perceived to be one, without any separation.

Oversoul: The oversoul resides in the non-material seventh density. Within the oversoul, all knowledge of all lifetimes, past, present and future can be found. In this density we can access our individual and collective Akashic records where all thoughts, emotions, sensations and memories from all lifetimes are recorded for all of eternity.

Pleiadians: Fifth dimensional star beings from the Pleiades constellation. They are master artisans, musicians and healers who value peace above all else.

Power Animal: A power animal is the energy of a particular animal that lives within you. Everyone has at least one power animal. Entering into trances to allow your power animal to dance and play will keep it happy. If you don't exercise your power animal, it will leave you.

Psychic Channels: Direct communication, third eye, message centre and direct knowing are the four energetic channels that enable you to receive psychic information.

Qi: Spiritual or formless energy. In Chinese medicine and Taoism you often hear of the three treasures which sustain human life: shen, qi, and jing. Qi is the template for all life. It is non-material, but manifests all matter. Correlates of qi are biochemical processes, bioluminescence and consciousness. Qi is often associated with a correlate, electricity. For this reason, the energy observed and utilized by Qigong practitioners is usually spoken of as a form of electrical energy. It is also known as prana in the yogic tradition.

Qigong: Qigong is an ancient Chinese martial arts and healing modality over thousands of years old. It usually involves a moving meditation with slow movements and relaxed breathing.

Sirians: Fifth dimensional star beings from Sirius star system. They are master healers, engineers and musicians who value imagination above all else.

Salamander: A fire spirit that can usually be found near fire.

Soul: The non-material part of you that stays with you through every lifetime. No tragedy can ever affect your soul. Your soul can never be hurt or lost. Your soul comes from Source and will eventually return there.

Soul Contract: Energetic cords created between two souls unconsciously or consciously that keep them bound together on a spiritual level. Holding onto anger directed at another person keeps a soul contract alive. To end outdated soul contracts, forgive your enemies and let go of toxic emotions.

Soul Detour: When you stray from your true soul path, you make a soul detour. Soul detours happen for a reason and always make you stronger.

Soul Group: A group of souls created together from the oversoul who share a collective mission or theme.

Source: Another word for God, the creator of all life. Everything manifests from the same Source, which is non-material and eternal.

Source Consciousness: Another word for God or Source.

Spirit: Another word for God or Source. Spirit can also refer to your soul or the spiritual realm.

Spirit Guide: Spirits which guide you to make decisions in alignment with your soul. Often spirit guides are friends from other lifetimes or deceased family members.

Sprite: A water spirit that can usually be found near rivers or lakes.

Starseed: A person who feels like they've lived lives in other star systems or on planets other than Earth.

Star Beings: Entities that exist within higher densities that act as spirit guides for the people of Earth.

Superfood: Foods that are jam-packed with vitamins, protein, good fats and antioxidants. They provide you with all your essential nutrients while boosting your immunity, energizing your body, enhancing your mood, and cleansing and alkalizing your system. As they work to provide you with proper nutrition they help maintain the homeostasis of your body, keeping your mood and energy levels balanced.

The Now: The present moment where you are fully empowered and connected to Source.

True Soul Path: The path in alignment with your heart's desires. You know you're on this path when you feel happy, energized and free. Straying from your true soul path will make you feel sad, tired and enslaved.

Unity consciousness: Another word for God or Source.

Unmanifest: The non-material, spiritual realm.

Venusians: Fifth dimensional beings from Venus. Masters of natural law and cosmic order, they value beauty and harmony above all else.

Introduction

There's a reason you picked up this book, and I don't believe in coincidences. Do you? Maybe, like most of us on the planet, you're frustrated and can't seem to stop thinking. Maybe you're suffering from a dis-ease and traditional healing modalities just aren't cutting it. Maybe you're just confused about life. Why did you come here? Who are you? Does any of this actually mean something? Maybe you're a seeker, interested in spirituality, ready for more, ready for the truth.

Perhaps you thought that this was a science fiction novel. I assure you there's nothing fictional about it. I also assure you that this book is like nothing you've ever read. It's not another New Age gimmick that spoon-feeds you sugar-coated truths and leaves you exactly where you were before.

This self-help book will help you get in touch with your true self: the part of you beyond the veil of ego that is fearless, creative, passionate, blissful and free. Merging with that aspect of yourself will take hard work and a commitment to the truth, but it can be simple if you keep an open mind and follow the exercises contained within this book.

If you're ready to take 100% responsibility for your life and claim your divine sovereignty, fantastic, keep reading. If you want to keep blaming your problems on external circumstances or people, you may as well put this book down. You're probably not ready for it yet.

Are you still here?

Good, let's continue. You didn't receive a manual titled, *How to be a Good Human* when you arrived here on Earth. If you've been looking for one, look no further than here.

This book contains nine sections which are designed to take you through an alchemical transformation. After this introduction, you get to learn about my journey in life and how I became a spiritual teacher. If you don't know me yet, my name is Christina Martine, and it's a pleasure to meet you. After working with countless clients, I've learned that we all essentially want the same thing: happiness. More specifically, the safety and freedom to express ourselves that naturally arises when we know who we truly are.

After a glimpse into my life, you'll read part one of this book, which explains Fifth Dimensional Healing, a technique that was channelled to me from my higher self. If you're not sure what the fifth dimension is, what channelling is, or what the higher self is, I've included a glossary at the beginning of the book for you to reference.

Part two focuses on healing the body. Is bread actually bad for you? Which fats keep you energized and which ones make you sluggish? How do you remove heavy metals from your body? How can you cleanse your organs properly and feel energized?

Part three focuses on healing the mind. How does meditation heal the brain? Is channelling dangerous? How can you start communing with spirit guides? Is magic real and how can you start manifesting your dream life using it?

Part four focuses on healing the emotions. How can you safely release trauma stored deep within your body? What's the difference between soul mates and twin flames? What does it mean to love yourself? What is sacred sex?

Part five focuses on healing the spirit. How can you strengthen your intuition and step into your psychic genius? What is astrology and does it take you away from your free will? What is your power animal and how can it help you? Why the heck did you choose to incarnate here anyway?

Throughout this book I make references to the various star beings I work with: the Venusians, Arcturians, Pleiadians and Sirians. These are higher dimensional entities or collectives from whom I receive information via my open psychic channels. Whenever you see meditations or transmissions from these entities, you're reading channelled material. No, I'm not special. I've just spent a long time doing energy healing practices to hone my natural gifts. You can do this too and if you keep reading, you'll see how easy it is to connect with your own team of spirit guides.

If you've never heard of channelling before or are skeptical of spirituality in general, feel free to put this book down and continue with your day. But if there's something stirring within you, a yearning deep inside that desires a genuine connection to your own soul, I invite you to read on.

You don't have to agree with everything in this book. In fact, it would be strange if you did, as you're on your own unique journey. I do encourage you, however, to keep an open mind and heart while reading. If a passage makes you come alive with curiosity or excitement, explore that excitement!

May this book serve as a catalyst on your healing journey and remind you of what you truly are: a divine being with limitless power and potential to create.

This book can't solve your problems for you, but it might show you where you're blocking your own flow of magic and miracles. It will be your choice to use the information provided to step into your true power as a creator.

Are you ready to make that choice?

Biography

I was an extremely curious, introverted and sensitive child, often preferring to live in the world within my mind over the one so many people kept assuring me was real. I grew up in a strict, loud and usually angry household, so I learned at a young age that the real world was dangerous. There were moments of peace, of course, afternoons whiled away creating worlds with words. In my stories, magic existed. Images of a place so breathtakingly beautiful swirled in my mind as my pencil danced along paper. My body shook with remembrance and soon it began to dawn on me that what others thought was simply my imagination was something entirely different: glimpses into alternate realities.

My strongest channelled memories were from another lifetime in a higher dimension. I could see myself there as a tall elf-like humanoid with scintillating skin and a golden aura. I was dressed in a long white robe and possessed the ability to work directly with the elements of nature, moving wind or water with my will alone. All senses heightened and tuned to the quality of a master artisan, I could sing with perfect pitch, emitting only the highest frequencies of God to heal the world. Every step I took was filled with grace, presence and power. I existed in harmony with the natural world and could speak directly to the animals and plants, but my lifestyle was far from rugged. The technology I used was infinitely more advanced than anything we have on Earth at present. Ornate crystalline buildings that mimicked the fractal unfolding of consciousness sparkled across the land, perfectly interwoven with the environment. These structures served as homes, natural energy generators and healing centres. There was no money in this world and no reason to commit any crimes. With so much beauty present, the desire simply wasn't there.

I would spend hours looking into this shimmering world with perfect clarity. After teaching myself meditation at age 13, I began to not only view this place with my third eye, but travel there astrally to receive insights and messages from higher dimensional beings. Despite my growing spiritual abilities and efforts to escape, the darkness of the real world overcame me.

I felt the anger—present during my formative years—deeply within every cell of my being, especially when my father and mother would fight. As an empath, someone who can absorb the emotions of others, both good or bad, I often mistook their pain as my own. I felt shame, regret and sorrow that wasn't mine, but I didn't know how to make it go away. As a result, I thought there was something wrong with me.

After my parents split when I was three, my younger sister and I lived with my mother, who was severely depressed and unable to let go of the past. She had always been naturally intuitive and tuned into the spirit world, a gifted psychic, though with little knowledge of how to use her gifts. Her refusal to let go of her identity as a wounded victim of the world around her, in combination with her deep sense of self-hatred, was projected onto me constantly. Her lack of empathy along with her heightened psychic perception caused her to scream statements at me that scarred my soul.

Now as an adult, I see that she was only projecting her own insecurities onto me. Her service-to-self attitude and inability to cope with human emotions invited many demonic entities to exist within her. I didn't know it as a child, but my house was riddled with demonic forces.

Demons are lower dimensional entities that can't exist physically with us, but can enter our energetic fields to feed off our fear. They do not offer and receive love the way most humans do and often are attracted to people who are unconscious of their own power. Those holding onto negative emotions, addictions or attachments are prime targets. A demon will find a person to exist with and then use that person's will to incite pain or fear in others. Empaths usually become the demon's main food source. The person afflicted with the demonic attachment will unconsciously be drawn to attack the empath to transform the empath's love into fear, to allow the demon to feed. The host of the demon feels a temporary power when feeding the demon, which inspires him/her to create more fear to feed off.

It's only when we choose to hold onto negative emotions or thoughts that demons can exist within us. When we forgive ourselves, all our enemies and choose compassion, we find our true alignment with Source energy, which is always loving.

I was livid with my mother for years. I would shake uncontrollably with fear and anger when she would enter the same room—scared that she would flip on a dime and strike me physically or worse, spiritually. It was her words that cut the deepest. I questioned constantly, "How can someone who is supposed to love me more than anyone be so cruel to me?" I kept this mentality for years, repeating the cycle of victim mentality, until one day I had had enough.

When I was in my early twenties, I decided that I wasn't going to be a victim of my past any longer. I stopped blaming other people for problems that weren't even mine. I forgave my enemies because I saw that they only lashed out because they too were suffering, trapped in a state of delusion, deeply unconsciousness.

Though my mother was there for me financially, growing up with her was hell-on-earth at moments. I cursed God for putting me through such torture, but I had enough awareness to know that others had it worse than I did.

I was never angry with my father because he had never been cruel to me in the same way my mother had been, but I felt like I couldn't rely on him for support because he too was dealing with his own mental health challenges and addictions. The divorce left him depressed and as a result he turned to alcohol to numb his pain.

Looking back now, I can say that I never truly felt like a child. I always had a maturity to me, perhaps because I had to learn how to care for myself at such a young age.

Though I had loving grandparents and friends, I always kept my distance emotionally, afraid that if I opened up too much to people, they would hurt me. I felt alone in an overpopulated world. Humans seemed like a cancer on the Earth, a sickness.

At age 17, I fell into such a deep depression that I decided I was going to kill myself. I took whatever pills I could find in the medicine cabinet. My mother had been a nurse for years and advocated the use of pharmaceuticals. The night of my birthday, I popped over 30 random pain killers and antidepressants that I found in the medicine cabinet. I genuinely believed that the world was an awful place and that I would never be able to relate to anyone. Being vulnerable was too terrifying; it had only ever brought me pain. I suppose I wanted to get revenge on my mother as well. Maybe my suicide would make her understand how much pain she had caused me. I lay on my living room couch as my reality shapeshifted and spun uncontrollably. I watched the blurry neon numbers on my VCR, and prayed to God to live. I moved in and out of consciousness all night, threw up in the morning, and here I am.

After my attempt, I had my first intense channelling experience. This wasn't like the long meditative journeys I would take myself on to have tea with my spirit guides. My astral travels, in dreams and in meditations were vivid, but there was a lightness to them. This was something entirely different. Energy more powerfully loving than anything I'd experienced thus far flooded into my crown chakra. I fell to my knees, crying with ecstasy and deep sorrow for what I had done, as a voice told me calmly, "Christina, you came here for a reason. If you kill yourself, you'll have to come back." Later I realized that this voice was my own, the voice of my fifth dimensional higher self. I was informed that I had many aspects of my being to call upon and all were existing simultaneously with the one I called Christina.

It became very clear to me that I had come to Earth to experience exactly what I was experiencing: to grow and heal.

My memory was activated over time and I realized that I was not of the Earth, but yes, I was meant to be here. As a starseed, someone who clearly remembers living within higher dimensions of consciousness, it was apparent that I had chosen to incarnate on Earth to hold space for others to heal and return to their natural state of enlightenment. The full awareness of my mission, however, was brought about through intense suffering. Pain was the only thing strong enough to wake me up and back into the remembrance of who I truly was.

After my first major awakening, or remembering, I still found it difficult to navigate. I had severe obsessive-compulsive disorder, a symptom of the abuse I suffered. Repeating things over and over to myself in my head, counting things or touching things in a specific way, brought me a sense of control. So did starving myself or purging my food, or abusing myself with drugs and alcohol. I knew I needed help and I prayed to my angels for healing.

My prayers were answered in the form of the book, *The Power of Now*, by Eckhart Tolle. As I read the book, my next major awakening occurred. I could clearly see that I was not my thoughts. I was a consciousness using my body, brain and heart as tools. I didn't have to obey my thoughts as if they were gods. They were just thoughts and usually not even mine.

Letting go of toxic thoughts took years and meditation was my medication throughout the process. As a young adult, I returned to my meditation practice and forced myself to sit and observe my mind, to do nothing. I had to remind myself that there was more power in surrender than in adhering to the ego, which was obviously fragmented. Why would I give my most precious commodity, my energy and attention, to something that didn't care about my well-being? My mind was insatiable and only meant to be a tool, nothing more. I didn't have to punish myself nor my body for not being able to live up to the endless demands of my own mind. What foolishness!

Learning to live without constantly referring to my mind for the truth was almost unbearable at first, but with my meditation practice I finally found peace. One day, after a long journey into the depths of my consciousness, simply sitting and breathing, I opened my eyes to discover that I couldn't remember what I had been obsessing about for months on end. I found strength that could not be created with thought. I saw that the truth of my being couldn't be comprehended at all. I couldn't fit the totality of who I was into a label. I couldn't quantify God. Life wasn't meant to be understood and neither was I. The more I learned to let go and trust in life, the more powerful I felt. All other forms of power were weakness disguised as strength. Control was a delusion I had created to feel temporarily safe but surrender was the path to freedom.

As my spiritual practice deepened into my twenties, I could clearly discern that I was an energetic being, an awareness that could observe life without any need to understand, justify or label it. As I sat with my mind gone temporarily, time-and-time again I witnessed that even with no identity, there was still something leftover: an awareness, a loving presence that never left.

I didn't have to seek love from others. I didn't have to cry with loneliness or despair over not having enough of it. I was love itself and the way to return to feeling that love was to give it away freely. Vulnerability wasn't a weakness. An open heart was the greatest strength in the world.

I saw that I was not a girl, not even a human at my core. I was truly formless, an emanation of love, everywhere all at once. I was connected to every other person. There was no separation. With this level of awareness, I could clearly see that even my mother who I had blamed my pain on for so long was a part of me. She too needed love. She had only forgotten that she too was also love, not just her personality or passing emotions.

Because nothing was separate from me, I became painfully aware that the abuse I had endured as a child was chosen by me to help me grow. If all was one and love was the only thing that truly existed, then everything that happened to me actually happened *through* me to return me to my power, to remind me of the truth.

I saw that I had chosen to experience total dis-empowerment in order to triumph over it. Without the awareness of what total dis-empowerment was, I wouldn't have been able to appreciate and use my power to help others heal. With patience and persistence my heart softened and I found the power of forgiveness. I saw that my enemies were only victims of the conditioning of a sick society that bought into the illusion of separation.

I began to realize that no one on Earth knew where they were, who they were or why they had come here. Most people had forgotten that they were magnificent beings of light. Our education systems dumbed us down with fake history and indoctrinated us with useless information that only enabled us to have the illusion of freedom. Being able to choose what job to work at for the duration of a life, within a dysfunctional slave system, was not freedom.

There was no other choice but to share my enlightenment with the world. I began making YouTube vlogs, offering my ideas to help others heal and see the greater truth. I wanted to make it clear that enlightenment was not something we had to search for. It was available to us in all moments and the way to get there was to turn inward. Remaining the witness, observing without thought, connected us to the Source of *all* that would never leave us. God is not in some far-off land watching over our every move, judging us for being sinners. God is within us, within everything. We are inherently good beings who may have only lost our way, distracted by the chaos of the physical world.

I could no longer subscribe to the eternal quest for happiness external to myself. While I still enjoyed the pleasures of the physical world, I knew that temporary pleasures would always turn to pain. Venturing deeper into my own consciousness brought me more joy than anything the external world could offer and I began learning Qigong with a master in my city.

When my sister went through her first mental breakdown, I experienced more pain than I had ever felt before. My heart sank with sorrow and confusion. Before then, I had never known that it was possible to lose someone before death. Diagnosed with bipolar disorder, I saw her go in and out of hospitals, on various pharmaceuticals. She would be fine for a month, or maybe a year, then go off her meds and lose her mind. Watching her personality shift into something unrecognizable was extremely challenging for me to witness. She would have intense delusions about people wanting to hurt her. On Thanksgiving 2016, handcuffed and forced to the ground by two police officers, she screamed at the top of her lungs that my mother was storing dead bodies in the trunk of her car. Even after the police officer checked just to make sure and obviously found nothing, she continued to scream the delusion from the top of her lungs, desperate to protect her ego. It was a memorable holiday to say the least.

Once again, I questioned why I had to witness people in such deep pain, but with my level of awareness, I knew that this was actually helping me step into my role as a healer and spiritual teacher on Earth.

I saw that everything is temporary and the tragedies of the material world can never affect the soul. The soul is eternal, impervious to the trauma accumulated with lifetimes past. Our cells, DNA, energetic channels and organs might be affected, but never the soul, the *one consciousness.*

Once again it was pain that pushed me further into my alternative healing practice. I could clearly see that there was a flaw in our medical system. Doctors prescribed pharmaceutical drugs to alleviate symptoms but didn't always cure dis-eases. The root of most physical ailments come from spiritual blockages, traumas from childhood stored deep within our energetic channels, past life scars trapped in cellular memory. After being introduced to Traditional Chinese medicine, I saw that the body is truly a holistic energetic field. You are not a machine that needs to be oiled up. You are a garden that needs tender loving care to blossom eternally. With the guidance of my higher self, I learned that DNA and the brain can be re-programmed, that you have the power to heal yourself. All you have to do is make the decision to heal, which isn't always easy. It's scary to take full responsibility, to not have anyone to blame.

All the psychiatrists my sister saw could not help her heal because her sickness did not originate within her mind. Her heart was closed-off and as a result her mind was distorted, her perception askew. She, like most of the women in my family, was also a gifted psychic with little knowledge of how to control her gifts.

I didn't want anyone to go through what my sister and I had gone through, so I began offering healing services to anyone who felt drawn to me. My videos were getting more popular on YouTube and I was making a name for myself in the online New Age community.

In sessions, I reminded clients again-and-again to not take things personally. Maybe I was also reminding myself. My purpose was simple. Whatever my heart yearned to express was what God intended for me to do. Whatever arose before me was there for me to offer love to, for all was me. All was an aspect of God and deserved the highest love.

As I helped people make the choice to heal, I too was healing. I saw that the sensitivity and deep empathy I had cursed for the majority of my life was in fact a gift meant to be shared.

Trusting in my intuition, I created the online community and social media site www.entersatoria.com. I wanted to continue to explore my own consciousness in the safety of a private community with like-minded souls ready to step into the fourth density.

In order to reach more people, I sit here now in Siem Reap, Cambodia, at age 28, writing the introduction to this novel. It is with the highest love, gratitude and respect that I offer this channelled material to you in hopes that it will awaken you to who you truly are.

February 5th, 2017

PART 1

Fifth Dimensional Healing Explained

Fifth Dimensional Healing is a holistic healing modality channelled from the fifth dimension by Christina Martine. The practices involve meditation, visualization, breathwork, energy healing, channelling and intention. Using Fifth Dimensional Healing, participants will draw their fifth dimensional selves into their energetic system to heal. Celestial guides from the fifth dimension are often called upon for assistance as well.

Sirian Transmission on Healing

In order to grasp the concept of healing on a non-material level, it's paramount to examine the difference between dimensions and densities. Densities can be seen as areas of consciousness and dimensions, the aspects therein. The densities can be correlated to the chakras within the human body. To make this intake of knowledge especially easy to digest, we shall stick to seven densities to align with the most commonly known seven chakra system.

Within the first density we find the elements, minerals and electricity, the building blocks of life, the foundation for all physical matter. The elementals can be called upon to assist in the evolution of your own soul and to balance your energies. The exact place in space and time you chose to be born into this world will determine the elemental structure of your energetic body. No one on this planet within fifth dimensional consciousness was born completely elementally balanced, and thus must take the proper precautions to balance their fields. The elementals love working with humans and can be utilized with the practice of energetic healing and intention.

In the second density we find the majority of the plants and animals. We say the majority because of course some of the animals on your planet Earth are observably more intelligent than the humans who have fallen back into unconsciousness because of the deception, lies and brainwashing of the mainstream media. Your dolphins still maintain their connection to our sixth density consciousness. We find our creative impulse and sexual desire begin to awaken in the second density.

In the third density we find humans at a more basic level of consciousness with self-awareness and primal instincts, but lacking greater knowledge of the self. The first three densities contain four dimensions of height, width, depth and time. In the third dimension, time and space are one and thus linear.

Moving onto the fourth density, we find our current human beings, of which many have now mastered love. In order to fully exist within the fourth density, one must have an open heart chakra. It is important to note that all beings on Earth currently have the capability to enter into the fourth density by choosing to offer love rather than remain in a fear-based illusion. Up until the fourth density, however, entities can still remain in service-to-self mode. The fourth density is an emotional realm where the lure of the ego still endures. Beyond the fourth density, the light of awareness prevents those from choosing anything other than actions that serve the good of all. It is true now that on your planet, most humans are entering from the third density into the fourth density. The fifth dimensional Earth plane will no longer be inhabited by third density humans who cannot grasp a greater understanding of compassion for all souls as one consciousness. Some newer souls will not be harvested into the next phase of evolution so eagerly awaited by those already awakened. Do not pity these souls, for this is simply their path. Not worse nor better. These particular souls, who either have more learning to do, or who have neglected their studies, will be transferred to another Earth-like home or another similar timeline to finish their third density cycle. As all souls have free choice, they may choose to continue to remain in the illusion of separation for as long as they please, but inevitably, the pain they inflict upon their own souls will force them awake.

In the fifth density we find yet higher beings who would not appear physical to third density humans, but would to one another. It is in this density that we master love on an even deeper level and step confidently into our magical abilities of instant manifestation. Only when one desires to manifest from a place of purity for the benefit of all can one exist harmoniously in this density.

In the sixth density, one can access profound wisdom and knowledge of the universe. Within the fifth or sixth density is where one finds her higher self, as you like to call it. This higher self is nothing other than a future version of you with a greater awareness of self. In the larger perspective, this higher self and your present self are not separate, as all that occurs is one. The higher self can be called upon for guidance at any time through simple intention alone. There are many higher selves that currently coexist with the consciousness focused in your present self. The fourth, fifth and sixth densities are fifth dimensional containing height, width, depth and time that is fluid and separate from space.

Finally, we come to the seventh density where the oversoul can be found, which contains all knowledge of all lifetimes, past, present and future. In this density we can access our individual and collective Akashic records where all thoughts, emotions, sensations and memories from all lifetimes are recorded for all of eternity. The seventh density does not contain any dimensions and remains non-material. Thoughts and emotions do not require a medium to travel through, and from the fourth density and beyond, are easily sent and received from many different planes of existence, even instantaneously.

Because of the separation of time from space within fifth dimensional consciousness, fifth dimensional beings, including you reading this transmission, can indeed travel with your astral body to the seventh density oversoul to retrieve information regarding past, present or future lives. This can be easily done through entering the heart through meditation. All chakras are gateways into the various densities of consciousness, the heart chakra being one of the easiest entrances into your personal Akashic records along with the collective ones. An awakened crown chakra may enable you to receive directly from the Akashic records also.

It is important to note that you also have several bodies that you enjoy living in. A lot of people on your planet currently have a body, but do not live in it for the majority of their time, instead preferring to live in the mental or emotional body. It is paramount for humans to open the heart chakra, also enabling them to access their astral bodies to travel in the fifth dimension, unencumbered. The exploration of the higher chakras will enable all to access the higher realms of existence and to do so consciously.

The activation of the light body is another subject we would like to address through this channel. Death has never been anything to fear as it is, of course, only a transition, though when you remain unconscious of your light body used to travel astrally, when you die you will enter into a void and have little control over what you witness. It is likely that you'll be cycled back into reincarnation where you will learn to raise your vibration and step into your true divinity. You will likely return to the Earth without your memories. During a resurrection, you die with an awareness that you do indeed have a spiritual body that is just as real as the one you've become so attached to. With the awareness of your light body, you move consciously into an area of consciousness and no longer have to reincarnate on Earth unless you choose to. Your memories remain intact. During an ascension, you remain completely aware and leave the Earth fully conscious to enter into a higher plane with all your memories. There is no time spent in the holding area. You enter immediately into a higher plane and no longer have to incarnate unless you so choose.

This knowledge is not shared to create fear, but to inspire further exploration into the nature of your own consciousness. Even with the slightest awareness that you are not your mind, that you are indeed an energetic being, you will not be unconsciously cycled back into reincarnation. You will have the choice about where and when you will go next.

Holding Space

Before I begin any healing session, I make sure that I'm in a very calm and centred space. After a meditation, I call upon my client's guides of the most superlative order to speak the words my client needs to hear through me. Let's say I'm talking to Mary. When I enter into the session, the first thing I do is ask Mary to close her eyes and place a hand over her heart. I ask her to ask herself, "How am I feeling?" and "What do I need?" When Mary feels relaxed, we set an intention for our meeting. I ask a few questions about what's going on in her life. I learn what her health is like, what she does for exercise and what she eats during a typical day. I ask her if she takes any vitamins, medication or supplements and discover how much alcohol and caffeine she consumes. From this it's very easy to discover where physical blockages may be coming from. I find out what she does for a living and ask her if she enjoys her career or not to quickly learn whether she's living in alignment with her higher self and walking her true path or not. I go into her love life and past relationships, focusing in particular on how they ended. Usually, unresolved childhood traumas can be spotted in recurring relationship drama. I briefly inquire about her upbringing and parents to see if there are any illnesses in her family. Then I ask her what she truly wants more than anything and why. I finish by asking her about what currently annoys her most and why.

As Mary speaks I watch how she holds herself, how she breathes and discern from observation whether she's in a receptive or contracted state. I observe Mary's eyes to see whether they're twinkling with life or tired from stress. I listen with my full attention. With my ears, I observe her pattern of speech and notice whether she puts herself down or has a healthy sense of pride. With my heart, I discern if the energetic vibrations coming from her lips are honest or not, whether she's choosing to speak from abundance or lack. With my body and Mary's permission, I temporarily tap into her energetic field and allow her greatest excitement or sorrow to become my own. This will result in personalized feelings of pain that are not my own which help me discern where stagnant energy is. I tune into her heart chakra to see whether it's open or shut off from the world because of past pain. With my psychic vision, I look into her energetic body to see if any chakras are blocked, and I read her aura to see how healthy and vibrant her energy is flowing.

As Mary continues to speak, her guides will often also be speaking to me through my psychic channels. Through my direct knowing channel, located at the navel and running in a straight line to the spine at the back, I'll receive instant knowledge from the divine to give to her. With my crown chakra, Source energy and information from her guidance team will pour into my physical vessel, which will be interpreted by my open heart chakra and mind. Along with this, my third eye will start to receive images about Mary's soul journey, where she's previously had incarnations, what star systems her soul has passed through, what her mission is, where her soul wants to go and what kind of karma she has to clear. These images come in flashes and I see them over the physical reality we identify with most often. As I receive these visions, sometimes sounds, smells, tastes or textures will accompany them. As I continue to read Mary and receive her soul template on the deepest spiritual level, I tap into her personal Akashic records, which are accessible to anyone through the heart. If Mary's heart is closed off, her guides will pass along to me any pertinent messages that need to be brought to light.

As all of this is happening, my guidance team helps to prevent any unwanted entities or toxic qi from entering my field. As an empath, (someone who feels the emotions other people feel) and clairsentient, (someone who can feel those same emotions at a distance), sometimes I get overloaded with the pain or joy of my client. Whether I'm in person chatting with someone or talking via the internet, my guides help me make sense of the information I'm being presented with, reminding me that what I'm feeling isn't mine to hold onto, just there to observe.

As I continue to listen and chat with Mary, I don't think too much. As I've allowed myself to become a divine channel, the words that Mary is meant to hear for her healing effortlessly leave my lips; her guides often speak through me.

Đis-ease

All dis-eases arise as a result of a physical, emotional, mental or spiritual blockage. Physical blockages can usually be attributed to a poor diet and lack of exercise. Emotional blockages occur as a result of stored toxic emotions such as shame, guilt, anger or jealousy. Mental blockages form because of an over-attachment to negative thoughts or the personality. Spiritual blockages are energetic traumas from the past, in childhood, or sometimes in past lives.

When you go directly to the soul to do healing, your thoughts, emotions and physical body transform to reflect your healed inner world. Even physical ailments or chronic conditions can arise from negative emotions stored in organs or energy meridians. Sometimes they result from past life wounds that are still present energetically and stored within cellular memory. When you go to a traditional Western doctor and complain of an ache in your arm, the doctor is only trained to look at the physical. If you go to a psychiatrist and complain of incessant negative thoughts, the psychiatrist is only trained to look at the functions of the brain. Anyone can see how this is a flawed design in our healthcare system, as illness doesn't simply arise from one source. You are a holistic, energetic being and need to be treated as such.

A naturopathic doctor or Qigong master, for example, will take a complaint such as a pain in the arm and a cloudy mind and access it on every possible level. After questioning the patient and running a series of tests, she may come to find that the physical pain in the arm of a client is actually the result of stagnant energy within a particular channel, occurring because of an energy blockage in the heart which has, as a result, clouded the patient's ability to think clearly. The depression the patient is feeling, the lack of vitality and excitement for life, cannot be directly correlated to the pain itself.

Pain is never the problem. It arises as a symptom of something much deeper: a trauma that wants to be acknowledged and transmuted through love. It can be overwhelming to face pain, to feel it fully in order to learn from it and discern why it's there at all, but when you do, you free yourself from your own self-created prison. Even physical accidents arise to help you realign with your divine being.

In a society where children are told that feeling painful emotions is wrong or bad, it's easy to see why most adults still don't know how to manage their painful emotions or thoughts. Instead of questioning their pain and sending it love to help them heal, it's unfortunately still common for them to ignore pain or stuff it deep down inside their body. More often than not, this stuffing causes blockages within the root chakra, the foundational chakra most often associated with survival and money. No wonder the majority of the world is struggling to make ends meet! Of course, when you supress anything that wants to be acknowledged, it will find a way to rise up, but it does so in a twisted, sometimes harmful way. Illnesses occur, supressed pain turns into outbursts of anger or bouts of depression, which most then seek to medicate and supress even further!

This cycle has to end!

That ending can start now, with the realization that you can heal yourself by learning to show up fully in each moment, and send love to anything that occurs in your experience. Rather than viewing your pain as a nuisance, instead view it as a wise teacher here to help heal you and return to you to your own heart. Life will then begin to work for you, not against you.

What if butterflies rejected their natural metamorphosis because it was painful? They would never turn into beautiful butterflies! Growing isn't always comfortable, but if we avoid labelling our emotions as bad, suddenly we see that they were never bad to begin with—only there to realign us with our power.

God never offers us anything we can't handle.

Any pain can be transmuted to peace if you stop resisting it and fully immerse yourself in any sensation that is bothering you. When you do this, your pain can no longer hurt you. It becomes a sensation, not good or bad. It simply is, and is there to steer you back in the direction of the highest truth coming from your own heart, your connection to the divine. With a release of any resistance to the present moment, no matter how painful it is, you create space within yourself to feel into the truth of what the pain is trying to show you. If you feel deeply into any sensation in the body, it will eventually lead you back to the serenity and stillness of your being.

Sometimes this process can be terrifying to do alone, and that's where I step in. Even though I refer to myself as a healer, it's never me who is doing the healing. In fact, sometimes clients come to me who aren't ready to face their pain and that's okay. Even if they see no progress (which is rare), I don't take it personally. I'm simply there to help create a safe space for healing to occur in. I act as a catalyst and a channel for the divine to remind the client of the power she has within herself to heal. I offer the truth from my heart, and the wisdom from many lifetimes doing the same sort of work I'm doing now, but it's always the client's choice to stop viewing pain as a barrier to the bliss that is already within.

You are Not Your Thoughts!

Since we live in a world where we're encouraged to think from the moment we awake to the moment we shut our eyes, helping my clients release mental blockages is always a primary focus. Let's return to our hypothetical Mary once again. After her initial reading, I ask her what she really wants to be doing in life. Then I ask her why she wants to be doing those things. From the responses I get, I can discern if she's in tune with her own heart and determine whether she's creating a life in alignment with her will or someone else's. Then I ask her why she hasn't been doing the things she wants to do most. Listening to her with full attention, I start to glimpse into the underlying limiting beliefs causing her inactivity.

The most common limiting beliefs I've come across have been: *My ideas aren't worthy of being heard. People won't like the real me. If I try, I'll end up failing. I don't have enough time to do the things I love.*

For almost everyone, it boils down to, *I'm not good* enough, which is just a thought and as you know, thoughts can be changed.

To figure out where the negative thought pattern is stemming from, I ask my client a few more questions about the thought itself. Together we enter deeper and deeper into the thought until we get to what event initially caused the thought. By placing conscious attention on negative thinking patterns, you can tell your brain that you have the ability to either choose to give attention to the thought or not. Its power to affect you is taken away.

For example, if a client thinks she's not good enough, I'll ask her if she thinks that the thought is true, and if so, I'll ask her, "Why?" From this place we go even deeper, and more often than not, we discover that current negative thoughts are symptoms of an unresolved trauma from childhood. If the client is used to running from pain, negative thoughts and emotions arise to help her heal those traumas.

Sometimes the simple awareness that the thoughts which plague us originally came as judgments from an angry parent or ex-partner is enough for resistance to fade and healing to occur.

In all my sessions, I emphasize that thoughts are simply thoughts. Just passing reflections, and not always true. It may shock the client to discover that she's holding onto outdated and false judgments of partners, co-workers, siblings or other loved ones.

In general, people have become so used to attaching to every single thought that passes through their minds that the mere illumination that they can *choose* to not attach to those thoughts usually creates an extreme sense of relief. With the simple awareness of awareness itself, the healing process begins.

Negative Emotions Arise Because of Unresolved Trauma

Recurring limiting beliefs that won't seem to go away can usually be traced down to a particular event where the client feels that someone who she truly trusted was cruel to her. After digging into the negative thought to find out who abused the client, we work on going into the memory associated with the abuser, the situation or event that caused the trauma now manifesting as the limiting belief. It's important to remember that abusers are really just victims of their own negative programming. The pain they inflict on others usually has nothing to do with their victims, and instead is indicative of their own traumas, the relationship they have with their own minds and the past they cling to.

Has anyone ever lashed out at you for no good reason? This happens as a result of unprocessed karma, which is really just unprocessed trauma stored within the body. Outbursts of anger from people we care about do not illustrate how worthy we are of love or respect. They serve to remind us to not take anything personally. Humans get triggered by past pain and re-live it in order to heal it. The good news is that the more you enter into your own inner world to do trauma-clearing, the more love you send to your own heart, the less likely you are to get triggered by external circumstances or people. Even if you do, you see all pain arising as a beautiful process leading you back to unity consciousness, where all is seen as equal and sacred.

If our hypothetical Mary has the limiting belief, *I'm not good enough*, before we enter into the memory associated with the initial trauma, I'll ask her to really step into the feeling of not being good enough. To do this, I use my **Fifth Dimensional Healing Technique: It's Safe to Feel**.

5D Emotional Healing Technique: It's Safe to Feel

1. Sit in silence with your eyes closed and enter into a meditative state by consciously focusing on your breath.

If any thoughts arise, simply say internally *thought* or *thinking* and return to the constant in-and-out of your breath. The goal of the meditation is to become relaxed enough to enter into the theta brain wave state (3-8 Hz), the brain state usually associated with sleeping, but also deep meditation. It's in this state that you're able to access your unconscious, your traumas, fears and intuition. In this state, when you receive outside suggestions or do clearing work on yourself, it's more likely for you to actually benefit from the advice, as you'll be directly affecting your subconscious, which controls the conscious mind.

2. After entering into deep relaxation, it's time to focus on what's going on inside the body. Ask yourself, "How do I feel?" If there's unresolved trauma from your past, now is the time to face it. If a thought arises such as, *I'm not good enough*, question how that thought feels. If a feeling such as shame comes up for you, focus all your attention on that feeling. Discover where in your body that feeling is localized, where you're choosing to store it. If you discover that the feeling of shame is centralized in your chest for example, focus all your attention on that area. Place your focus in the centre of the shame located in your chest. Now tell it, "It's okay that you're here. You have a right to be here. You are worthy of being here. I love you."

This will instantly bring a lot of relief for most people as they've been so conditioned to supress negative emotions or view them as inconveniences when in reality they only arise to return us back to our own innocence. If you begin to cry, allow the tears to flow and know that we release toxins, fear, and cleanse the liver and anger through crying.

3. Continue to send love to the shame until you feel a release, a shift in energy. Then send out that feeling of shame into your entire body and tell it, "It's okay that you're here. You have a right to be here. You are worthy of being here. I love you." Doing this creates space for the feeling to move and transform. Once you feel another shift in energy, another release, send the feeling of shame out into the room around you and repeat the mantra: "It's okay that you're here. You have a right to be here. You are worthy of being here. I love you." Once another shift in energy is felt, send the shame out into the universe to leave your field once and for all, commanding it to be transmuted into love.

Repeat this process for any other negative emotions that arise to be healed. When you give yourself the safety and space to explore your negative emotions, and you have the courage to truly witness them without judgment, they always have a message to share, and that message always leads back to the heart.

A Conscious Journey of Self-Discovery

"The Fifth Dimensional Healing I did with Christina Martine was extremely comforting and empowering. She really holds space for people to feel safe so they can journey into places they never want to revisit again, but want to be liberated from. I was impressed how intuitively she was able adapt and cater to my needs when being in that vulnerable state. This healing method doesn't require you to be in hypnosis, or an unconscious state where you lack control. Instead it is a cooperative journey where you are completely aware of yourself and able to dive deep into your being. Christina acts as trustworthy guide, support, and navigator to help you on your journey of self-discovery. Sometimes all we need is a helping hand and for someone to be present with us as we take steps towards our empowerment and freedom. Having Christina with me to guide me through my healing journey was priceless!"

Hillmy Al-Abdulsalam, client

Talk to Your Emotions

If Mary finds that a particular emotional trauma won't seem to leave, we enter more deeply into that trauma. Once in a meditative state, I ask her to describe the emotion she's feeling and locate it for me in her body. Once she's found the location, I ask her if there's a colour or an image associated with the emotion. Then I ask her what the emotion wants. If Mary responds with, "Control," or something similar, I go deeper. I ask, "Is that all? What else does it want?" After digging into the negative emotion to find out why it's there at all, the truth, the desire to feel safe, or another positive emotion will eventually arise. I ask, "What would happen to the emotion if it had acceptance?" If Mary responds with, "It would calm down," or something similar, I move on to questioning how she would feel if she felt accepted. If she responds with, "Peaceful," I ask her what colour and images arise for the feeling of peace, along with, "What activities would you do if you felt peaceful?" Then I get Mary to breathe the new colour and images into the negative emotion. I ask her to concentrate on allowing the toxic colour and images to be completely absorbed by the new, peaceful colour and correlated images. On the exhale, I get Mary to send the peaceful energy into her body. She repeats this process until the toxic energy is completely absorbed by the healing energy she's provided herself with through focused intention, attention, imagination and intuition.

In some cases, clients are absolutely terrified to face their negative emotions. They feel as if another entity is within them and if they allow themselves to feel the pain, the entity will take over. This is just the mind's way of tricking them out of presence. Whether clients have dark entities within them or not, running from them will not solve their problem. Facing it entirely and sending it love will allow the dark energy to dissipate and be transmuted back into love. Only when you run from your pain can it have any power over you. Dark entities or dis-ease cannot exist in a body filled with love.

⤬

Forgiveness = Freedom

Forgiveness is a major aspect of the healing process. In order to truly heal and step into your true power, it is absolutely necessary to forgive yourself for any mistakes you've made in the past, and forgive anyone who's hurt you. Remember, your abusers were doing the best they could with the state of consciousness and the amount of awareness that they had. When you enter deeply into your own pain and allow it to be, and stop viewing your pain as something negative, you give yourself the opportunity to forgive.

After explaining to my client my holistic view of the world, I ask, "Have you not forgiven someone for something? Are you holding onto any anger directed at someone else?" If we discover anger directed toward a particular person, I may choose to use my **Fifth Dimensional Healing Technique: Seven Golden Orbs of Light**.

Your consciousness is not limited to your body. The same awareness that exists within you also exists within the stars. By practicing the exercises contained within this book, you too will be able to connect to your celestial guides.

5Ɖ Arcturian Spiritual Ħealing Technique: Seven Golden Orbs of Light

Having someone guide you through this process is useful, as it can be emotionally overwhelming at times. Enter into a deep meditation where you have the ability to access your unconscious mind. Think of the negative emotion associated with the person you're angry at. Recall the event that initially caused the anger that resulted in stored trauma. Re-live the painful memory all over again in the safety of your mature body. If you were a child when the trauma occurred, see through the eyes of yourself as a child once more. Have the abuser enter into the situation and repeat whatever they did to you that caused you so much pain. Make the image as detailed as possible and really allow yourself to feel the pain you felt as a child. Succumb to the pain entirely within the safety of your adult body. Now have the abuser leave the room and invite your present self into the room.

Have your present self sit with you as a child and ask you to explain what happened. Still viewing the situation through the eyes of you as a child, explain how you're feeling, how much it hurts. Have your present self tell you, "It's okay for you to feel that way. Your feelings are valid. You have a right to feel that way. What happened to you is not your fault. I love you. You are safe."

Have your present self ask you what you need. If you need to be held and showered with affection, then create that scene. Have your present self give you any emotional, physical, spiritual or mental nourishment that you require. There are no limits to what you can manifest as you're working within the same area of consciousness you go to when you sleep. When you feel safe, have your present self offer a special healing gift to you.

Watch as your present self offers you seven golden orbs of light. Have your present self manifest the first golden orb of light and place it in your root chakra, located at your perineum. Then watch your present self place another golden orb into your sacral chakra, located just above your groin area. Watch as your present self places another golden orb into your solar plexus chakra, located at your navel area. Watch your present self place another golden orb into your heart chakra, located to the right of your physical heart, in the centre of your chest. Watch your present self place another golden orb into your throat chakra, located at your throat. Watch your present self place another golden orb into your third eye chakra, located in the middle of your forehead. Finally, watch your present self place the final golden orb into your crown chakra, which sits in the very centre of the top of your head and flowers out to receive spiritual energy.

As you sit glowing with the seven golden orbs within your body, watch as your present self activates each protective orb one-by-one. Have your present self activate the first orb by turning it bright ruby red. Listen as your present self tells you, "Your root chakra is now cleared, strengthened and fully activated. From the fifth dimension, I command you to be grounded, stable and financially secure now." With your awareness on your root chakra, repeat aloud, "Your root chakra is now cleared, strengthened and fully activated. From the fifth dimension, I command you to be grounded, healthy, stable and financially secure now."

Have your present self then activate the second protective orb by turning it bright goldfish orange. Listen as your present self tells you, "Your sacral chakra is now cleared, strengthened and fully activated. From the fifth dimension, I command you to be creative, sexually healed and empowered to create from unity consciousness now." With your awareness on your sacral chakra, repeat aloud, "Your sacral chakra is now cleared, strengthened and fully activated. From the fifth dimension, I command you to be creative, sexually healed and empowered to create from unity consciousness now."

Have your present self then activate your solar plexus chakra, turning it bright sunshine yellow. Listen as your present self tells you, "Your solar plexus chakra is now cleared, strengthened and fully activated. From the fifth dimension, I command you to be confident, assertive and proud to be human now." With your awareness on your solar plexus chakra, repeat aloud, "Your solar plexus chakra is now cleared, strengthened and fully activated. From the fifth dimension, I command you to be confident, assertive and proud to be human now."

Have your present self activate the golden orb at your heart chakra next by turning it bright emerald green. Listen to your present self say, "Your heart chakra is now cleared, strengthened and fully activated. From the fifth dimension, I command you to love your own heart, to be fearless and to align your will with the will of

God now." With your awareness on your heart chakra, repeat aloud, "Your heart chakra is now cleared, strengthened and fully activated. From the fifth dimension, I command you to love your own heart, to be fearless and to align your will with the will of God now."

Watch your present self activate the next orb by turning it bright sapphire blue. Have your present self say, "Your throat chakra is now cleared, strengthened and fully activated. From the fifth dimension, I command you to speak clearly, honestly and to create only that which benefits all souls now." With your awareness on your throat chakra, repeat aloud, "Your throat chakra is now cleared, strengthened and fully activated. From the fifth dimension, I command you to speak clearly, honestly and to create only that which benefits all souls now."

Watch your present self activate the next golden orb of light by turning it bright vibrant indigo. Listen to your present self say, "Your third eye chakra is now cleared, strengthened and fully activated. From the fifth dimension, I command your third eye to open so you may see clearly with activated psychic abilities now." With your awareness on your third eye chakra, repeat aloud, "Your third eye chakra is now cleared, strengthened and fully activated. From the fifth dimension, I command your third eye to open so you may see clearly with activated psychic abilities now."

Have your present self activate the final golden orb by turning it bright shimmering violet. Listen to your present self say, "Your crown chakra is now cleared, strengthened and fully activated. From the fifth dimension, I command you to be a divine channel for Source consciousness, for you to exist in perfect health and to live and love in unity consciousness now." With your awareness on your crown chakra, repeat aloud, "Your crown chakra is now cleared, strengthened and fully activated. From the fifth dimension, I command you to be a divine channel for Source consciousness, for you to exist in perfect health and live and love in unity consciousness now."

Still viewing the scene through the child's eyes and breathing comfortably with all your chakras fully activated, deliver rainbow healing light into your body while exhaling. Listen as your present self tells you, "Your body is now cleared, healed, strengthened, protected and fully activated. You are now vibrant, healthy, blissful, peaceful and filled with divine light. From the fifth dimension I command you to exist in the eternal now with full awareness of your complete divine being." Viewing your form glowing with rainbow light, repeat, "Your body is now cleared, healed, strengthened, protected and fully activated. You are now vibrant, healthy, peaceful and filled with divine light. From the fifth dimension I command you to exist in the eternal now with full awareness of your complete divine being." Deliver the rainbow light into the room around you and beyond into the universe. Listen to your present self say, "Your reality is now cleared, healed, strengthened, protected and fully activated. You are now vibrant, healthy, blissful, peaceful and filled with divine light. From the fifth dimension I command you to be safe, loved and to exist in unity consciousness now." Surrounded in rainbow light repeat, "Your reality is now cleared, healed, strengthened, protected and fully activated. You are now vibrant, healthy, blissful, peaceful and filled with divine light. From the fifth dimension I command you to be safe, loved and to exist in unity consciousness now."

Bask in the beauty and perfection of the rainbow light for as long as you need to. When you feel ready, invite the abuser back into the room, with your present self standing by. You should feel no fear as you are now fully protected and channelling fifth dimensional protective energy, living in unity consciousness. Have the abuser apologize and explain herself to you. "I'm sorry. I wasn't aware that I was hurting you. I apologize from the bottom of my heart. Please forgive me for my mistake. Thank you for listening. I love you."

As the child, now forgive the abuser. If you feel like you can't, change the memory entirely so you can. Remember, we cannot change the past, but we can change how we view it and this act changes the present. It takes true courage to forgive our enemies, but it's the only way to completely heal and step into our full power.

If you still feel like you cannot forgive, simply send love to your own heart. Be honest. Speak aloud to your own heart, "I feel like I can't forgive. I love you. Thank you for healing me." In being so radically honest, more often than not, a great burden is lifted from us. Our energy shifts instantly and we come to find that we can indeed forgive. Don't worry about casting negative spells. Repeating out loud that you're afraid won't bring more fear to you. It will provide you with relief. Always focus on the emotions behind your words.

If forgiveness is still impossible at this point, which is rare after clearing the heart chakra, it's time to let go of the need to forgive entirely and simply continue to send love to your own heart. By doing this, by choosing to love yourself fully, your own heart forgives on your behalf.

If it's still difficult to look at your abuser, transform her into another version of herself that you can accept: a smiling, happy version that brings you peace, or perhaps a younger more innocent version that you can trust. If you can forgive now, do so. If not, hold the upgraded image in your heart and say, "I love you. I forgive you. Thank you for healing me."

You can now make amends by consciously choosing to re-write the memory in any way you see fit. If it feels right for you to go on a walk together, smiling and laughing, envision it. As you envision it, feel how filled with love and acceptance you are. Whenever it feels right to return to the present, say goodbye, and slowly open your eyes.

While in trance, you may find that the earliest memory of your initial traumas may not even be from this lifetime at all. You can repeat the same process above as you explore previous lives in meditation.

Become a Time Traveller

The programming that occurs during the **Seven Golden Orbs of Light** exercise is channelled from the fifth dimension.

Densities are areas of consciousness that we move into from Source. To visualize the densities, imagine life is a video game simulation. Every density that gets created from Source, all the way down to the first, is like a level you have to play through. We move from Source down to the first density to start the game. Then we move up through the densities back to Source to win the prize of eternal life with no suffering. Dimensions are the characteristics of the densities, or video game levels, of consciousness. Dimensions determine what the beings look and act like in each density and how they will respond to their environment.

The first three densities are fourth dimensional, where time and space is linear and difficult to manipulate. The fourth, fifth and sixth densities are fifth dimensional, where time and space is non-linear and much easier to manipulate. The seventh density and beyond is non-material and timeless. On Earth we are currently moving into the fourth density with fifth dimensional consciousness. This means we'll have much more ability to manifest our desires because we'll be closer to Source consciousness, which is the Source of all power.

If you're reading this book you've already made the choice to enter into the fourth density. As the information provided sinks in on a soul level, you may start to notice your perception of reality start to shift. This isn't something to be fearful of, but rather to rejoice in! If you find yourself no longer interested in things that used to bring you immense joy, this is perfectly normal! As you shift into becoming a fifth dimensional human, your entire outlook on life will shift too. Your fears, frustrations, desires and aspirations will change along with you. Breathe through any uncomfortable sensation and trust that your growing pains are leading you to a sense of peace beyond comprehension.

When you repeat the affirmations in the **Seven Golden Orbs of Light** as the child you actually invoke your fifth dimensional self to heal you. Your fifth dimensional higher self usually exists within either the fifth or sixth density and is not bound to space and time in a linear fashion. This self has much more power to create because it is much closer to Source.

Since time is an illusion we create to play within the video game that is life, you always have access to every life you're living simultaneously with this one. Because the trip back up to Source is inevitable, you know that you also already exist in the higher realms. You can call upon your higher self/selves at any time to exist with you here in the present. This channelling of energy enables you to make better decisions with a higher state of awareness and broader perspective.

When you enter into deep trance meditations to heal and visit memories from your past in order to change how you view them, this is a form of time travel. By healing yourself as a child and giving yourself the love and protection you need, you consequently jump to a completely different timeline in the present. Your entire reality changes in the present to become a vibrational match to the healed you. Since you know that time is flexible and that what was, what is, and what is going to be, is one when you travel on the astral plane to heal yourself, you bring that healed version of yourself into the present. It's clear to see that it's a choice to continue to live out past pain in the present, or to go directly to the past and change how you view it in order to manifest your present life from a place of purity.

5D Redo

If you're out in public and suddenly find yourself triggered by a past trauma, you can easily perform a simplified Fifth Dimensional Healing technique on yourself which I call a **5D Redo**.

To use myself as an example, I was eating dinner at a restaurant in Bali, Indonesia in 2017 and for some reason I was having trouble swallowing again. I used to get a strange psychosomatic response to stress where I would get scared to swallow my food, because I thought if I did I would choke and die. Completely irrational, but there it was. Instead of letting it completely destroy yet another beautiful meal, I thought: *Why not use 5D Healing on myself right now?*

I thought back to the very first time this strange response occurred. I was in the lunchroom on break from a job I knew I didn't belong at. Instead of listening to my intuition and leaving, I had stayed there, thinking that I needed the money, that I had no other options. Because of this, my heart chakra began to close slightly, and as a result, so did my throat chakra. I started to eat my lunch and found that I couldn't swallow. Every time I tried to, my chest would fill with fear and I would cough. My body was warning me that I was on the wrong path, but I still wasn't listening.

After finding the initial point of trauma (the first time it ever occurred), which I call the initial soul detour, I quickly changed how I responded to it. As I sat there at the restaurant in Bali, within my mind's eye I watched myself pack up all my things instead of heading back to work. I saw myself say goodbye to my boss and leave with no regrets. I felt the stress and anxiety from my chest leave and the tension from my throat loosen. I was back on my true soul path and realized the fear had only been there to help me home. I had performed a soul reroute on myself. By doing this I had changed the way my energy flowed within me, enabling me to shift into a more preferable timeline.

I opened my eyes at the restaurant and took a bite of food, swallowing effortlessly, my stress response gone entirely. To this day, it has not returned.

5D Redo Steps

To perform a quick and efficient **5D Redo** on yourself, take the following steps:

1. Find a quiet place to shut your eyes for a moment. If you're in a crowded place, head to a bathroom for some privacy. Take in some slow, deep breaths to get yourself in a meditative state.

2. Find the initial soul detour, the moment where you first remember experiencing the fear, anxiety, etc., that is still triggering you now.

If you want to perform a **5D Redo** and don't know your initial soul detour, enter into a meditation and allow your mind to wander back in time until it finds the oldest memory where the toxic energy you want released was present. Finding the oldest memory will often create space within your energetic field for more information to flow. Sometimes your true initial soul detour may be from another incarnation.

3. Re-live the painful memory, looking through your own eyes. Allow yourself to feel the negative emotions once more.

4. If you feel tension arise in your body, focus on it. It's there to be released. Take a deep breath in and imagine light from Source moving down toward you. Say, "I draw my fifth dimensional self into this (name the emotion) and transmute it to love throughout all densities, dimensions, time and space."

5. Re-watch the scene from an outsider's perspective. Detach yourself from the emotions that used to trigger you. Watch yourself act out the scene as if it wasn't you at all. Play the scene through like a movie. This will allow you to detach from the pain that used to trigger you. You can choose to replay the scene backwards in your head. You can speed it up and replay it over-and-over again to make it funny. Replay the scene until you don't see it as something negative, but rather just something that happened.

6. Now that you're comfortable with changing the memory and it no longer triggers you, you can perform a soul reroute. Continue to watch yourself from an outsider's perspective. What action would have returned you to your true soul path? What action would have been most in alignment with your heart? If your memory involves a person treating

you poorly, for example, instead of cowering in fear, stand up for yourself. See yourself loudly proclaiming, "Do not disrespect me!" If you're alone, scream it out loud! Feel the fear physically releasing from your body. Watch yourself leaving the presence of the other person for good and never returning. Do whatever you have to do to cut your soul contract with that person and reroute to a more preferable timeline.

7. Open your eyes to witness your new timeline. Offer a prayer of thanks to the divine for gracing you with such a powerful sense of awareness and the ability to heal.

Childhood Trauma Released

"Christina's Fifth Dimensional Healing techniques are powerful tools that helped me transform my life! I was amazed at how easy it was for me to let go and get into that deep theta state with Christina's guidance. I loved the 5D Redo so much, I often think of how to use it in my daily life. During a 5D Redo, I was able to go back to a memory which I hadn't realized had impacted my life so deeply: a childhood birthday party I hadn't thought of in years! It was there when I really first experienced guilt. I realized that guilt has prevented me from shining my light throughout most of my life. At the party, I accidentally hurt one of my friends because I was so excited to play with those popper toys that shoot confetti. I didn't realize they were so loud and by accident, I ended up hurting my friend's ear. When I attempted to apologize and reconcile, I was pushed away. I was so ashamed that I had hurt her. I went from having such a great time, to being demonized by everyone at the party. I was just a kid having fun and I didn't mean to hurt anyone! I wasn't aware that I had been carrying that guilt ever since. Through Fifth Dimensional Healing, I realized that the guilt I carried created a fear of expressing myself openly. In my adult life, I see this when I shy away from being the center of attention or when I choose to shine less brightly out of fear. Using this technique really allowed me to release that guilt and I feel much more comfortable in my own skin now. I visualized the party, re-wrote the reactions, and brought forgiveness to the situation. I highly recommend Christina Martine's 5D Healing techniques for everyone, as they truly are powerful and will help you transform your life."

Rochelle Bjorklund

www.newearthangelsascension.com

You are the Source

Soul detours happen for a reason and always make us stronger. We must never punish ourselves for straying from our path. We don't, however, have to let them ruin our lives.

When you become aware that you've taken a soul detour, simply reroute yourself back to your true soul path with a **5D Redo**. Although you cannot travel into the past with your physical body within the fourth density while using a **5D Redo**, you can travel to this density while using your light body or view it with your third eye. Some of the people on this planet are already actively living within the fourth density. Others will die and be reborn on a similar planet to continue to learn life lessons in order to enter the fourth density.

Within the fourth density you can send your energy to a specific area of consciousness or view that area with your third eye, and by doing so send the same energy. Viewing areas of consciousness without actually travelling there with your light body may be just as effective for you. When you send your energy to view another area of consciousness with your third eye, an energetic cord is created that stems from your third eye out to the place you're looking at. Your vital energy gets sent along this cord to the exact spot you're viewing. The energy that you're sending doesn't require a medium to travel through, so if your third eye is completely open, you will be able to send your energy instantaneously and receive insights as fast as your brain can interpret them. If you're third eye is only slightly open, the insights you receive may be cloudier or received and interpreted at a slower rate. Think of the energetic cord like a radio signal. The stronger the signal, the more easily the information can flow to you.

When you travel with your light body, or astral body, you actually leave your physical body to travel to another area of consciousness. Unencumbered by your physical form or the third or fourth density you're in, you're free to travel throughout all densities and dimensions, even back up to Source. Whether you can consciously do this now or not, nightly you travel to the Source and back to your body for healing energy.

Remember, all that is occurring is occurring at once within the moment, with no separation. Whether you perceive yourself to be a separate form moving through space and time or not, in your true form, which is formless, you are already connected to wherever you are trying to go or whoever you are trying to see. The movement you perceive is actually an illusion created by the mind. By going to the level of the soul with Fifth Dimensional Healing, you connect directly to the Source whether you perceive yourself physically moving or not.

The Source is always with you, and indeed it *is* you, in whatever form you choose to be in, regardless of where you choose to incarnate. You are always complete, regardless of whatever game of life you choose to live for fun. Out of the formlessness that you can never be separate from, arises qi/prana/life force energy, the template for all other forms of energy that you now perceive. Underneath the illusion of form, you are still formless and complete. This formlessness is what I also refer to as the Source, or God.

Within the fourth density most of us find ourselves in now, along with the fifth and sixth densities, we have fifth dimensional consciousness. With this consciousness, we can travel out-of-body using our light body through space and time, which is not linear. The Fifth Dimensional Healing work we do as we time travel changes the way our energy runs internally, which changes the external world we see.

Once again, we're not really moving at all. It just appears that we are. In truth, we are still the same formless presence which is complete. All apparent movement arises out of the eternal stillness that we come from, that we will always be.

You have the power to re-create yourself anew in any moment, for you are the creator itself!

PART 2

Heal Physical Blockages

Become a Formidable Toroidal Forcefield

Regardless of gender, nationality, race, religion, sexual orientation or beliefs, we all have something in common: a human body that requires proper nutrition to function. Your body, your form, is just as sacred as the formless, and indeed it's the physical body that is the vessel for Source consciousness to be brought into this world. Your body is a sacred spaceship that allows you to travel through dense realities, experiencing yourself as a separate being, in order to see your magnificence reflected to you as another. It's your body that allows you to play the video game that you call life on Earth and enables you to move through densities one through six.

When your body is supplied with nutritious food and water, your entire energetic system is able to flow harmoniously. You can then think peaceful thoughts and feel positive emotions, which in turn draw higher dimensional energy into your system. When your healthy habits become a healthy lifestyle, the continuous energetic downpour of celestial information—sending vibrant qi to all your cells—becomes a formidable toroidal forcefield. Qi moves so effortlessly through you that any negative attacks, whether physical, mental or otherwise, are filtered from your system almost instantly. So yes, your spiritual health, your true wealth, first does begin with your physical well-being!

Feel Vibrant Again

In the Western world, most of us were raised on a diet consisting of fruits and vegetables that were sprayed with pesticides, meat that was treated with antibiotics and milk that was full of hormones. We ate refined sugars and toxic grains—food that was highly processed and filled us up, but had little-to-no nutritional value. The consequence of this diet? No energy, a poor immune system and the inability to lose weight.

On top of our poor dietary habits, we were exposed to heavy metals through mercury amalgam fillings or vaccines, along with fluoride in our drinking water. *The Lancet*, one of the world's oldest and most prestigious medical journals has officially classified fluoride as a neurotoxicant.[1]

It's no surprise then that so many auto-immune disorders and chronic illnesses have appeared. Dr. John Matsen, ND, in his book, *Eating Alive 2*, states that:

> "Diseases like Alzheimer's, Parkinson's, amyotrophic lateral sclerosis (ALS—also known as Lou Gehrig's disease), cancers, strokes, heart attacks, diabetes, and hiatal hernias are assumed to be more common because the population is living longer.

---

[1] Dr. Philippe Grandjean, MD and Dr. Philip J Landrigan, MD, "Neurobehavioural effects of developmental toxicity," *The Lancet* 13 (2014): 3, http://dx.doi.org/10.1016/S1474-4422(13)70278-3.

The younger generation, however, also has a wide range of chronic health problems. Ten percent of young children now have eczema, and asthma and allergies are commonplace amongst youngsters. One out of 500 children has autism, and diabetes and cancer aren't rare in young children anymore. Dyslexia, hyperactivity, attention deficit disorder, and behavioural problems have made 20 percent of students in some areas learning-disabled.

The group between young and old has its own rash of health problems such as chronic fatigue, fibromyalgia, rheumatoid arthritis, reflux indigestion, acne, sinusitis, psoriasis, depression, anxiety, cancers, schizophrenia, manic depression, thyroid problems, ankylosing spondylitis, infertility, premenstrual syndrome (PMS), menstrual cramping, prostate enlargement, epilepsy, multiple sclerosis (MS), lupus, Crohn's disease, colitis, and irritable bowel syndrome."[2]

The good news is that you have the power to heal your body and even reverse the symptoms of chronic illness. To reclaim your vibrant physical health, you may have to implement several lifestyle changes. Along with learning to respond to stress in a positive way, some of the changes may include:

- Removing heavy metals from your body;
- Healing your liver;
- Improving good intestinal flora and eliminating intestinal yeast;
- Removing toxic grains from your diet;
- Eating a diet rich in nutrition;
- Increasing your oxygen intake;
- Getting a good night's rest.

---

[2]   Dr. John Matsen, ND, introduction to *Eating Alive 2* (North Vancouver: Goodwin Books, Ltd., 2002), p. xii.

Mercury Amalgams

The amalgam dental fillings, usually silver in colour, are made up of 50 percent mercury, the rest a combination of silver, copper and tin. Chelation research shows that the mercury continuously leaks from amalgam fillings and collects in the body, especially in the kidneys, liver and brain. This can cause a slew of health concerns, mental, emotional and physical. On a spiritual level, the mercury that collects in the brain clouds the third eye and makes connecting to spirit more difficult. This often results in severe depression.

In the presence of nearby gold fillings, mercury can be subject to galvanic action, which increases the release of mercury vapours. Hot or acidic foods or the brushing, grinding, or polishing of teeth can also increase the release of vapours.

Dr. Matsen states that when mercury is swallowed in salvia, it may:

> ". . . react with the hydrochloric acid (HCl) of your stomach, forming mercuric chloride. Mercuric chloride can kill off your beneficial intestinal bacteria, allowing the overgrowth of yeast, parasites, and harmful bacteria. Also, when mercury combines with the HCl of the stomach, there is less HCl available for the digestion of food, leading to heartburn, bloating, indigestion, and other digestive problems.[3]

> The bacteria and yeast in your mouth and intestine can turn methylate elemental mercury into methylmercury. Both methylmercury and mercury vapour that leaks from amalgam

---

[3]   Matsen (2002) *op. cit.* (note 2), pp. 3-4.

fillings can be major contributors to many of the 'mysterious' chronic physical, mental, and emotional illnesses—especially those that are neurological or immunological."[4]

Vaccines

Mercury in the form of thimerosol is used as a preservative in many vaccines. The hepatitis B and pertussis vaccines both contain thimerosol as a preservative.

No long-term studies on the safety of vaccines have ever been done. If vaccines are not mandatory in your country, you may choose not to have them. If you do choose to get vaccinated, refuse vaccinations containing the preservative thimerosol. Only elect to have vaccines when in good health. Supplement with vitamin C before and after the vaccine to alleviate adverse reactions.

Removing Heavy Metals from Your Body

Unfortunately, removing your mercury amalgams can be quite a long and expensive process. Before you invest in the actual removal of your fillings, make sure you strengthen your immune system and liver by cutting out alcohol, tobacco, coffee, refined sugars and grains. By eating foods rich in nutrition, and restoring the balance of your good intestinal bacteria, you can eliminate many of the symptoms of metal toxicity.

---

[4]   Matsen (2002) *op. cit.* (note 2), p. 4.

After the removal process, mercury may still linger in your body. You may opt for a chelation process by consuming DMPS, a sulfur compound that can be taken orally in capsule form or mixed into an acidic drink. Dr. Matsen notes, "DMPS circulates in the blood and chelates—binds—metals into very stable and non-toxic molecules that can be excreted primarily by the kidneys. Taking DMPS orally is recommended over intravenous administration."[5]

Chelation has to be performed with extreme care and caution as it may actually spill more heavy metals into the body if done improperly. Pregnant women should not perform chelation. If you are allergic to sulfur, you should inform the person administering the DMPS, so a trial dose can be taken first.

Along with a high-protein diet and colon hydrotherapy, some foods aiding in the chelation process include chlorella, garlic and cilantro. Chlorella, a single-celled green algae, and cilantro have both been proven to bind with heavy metals to help remove them from the body. Chlorella's molecular structure allows it to bond to heavy metals and chemicals in your digestive tract, which is your body's pathway to the bloodstream. Chlorella only binds to the unwanted metals in your body and leaves behind the beneficial minerals such as calcium, zinc and magnesium. Cilantro helps remove metals from the central nervous system through the urine. Garlic contains compounds called sulfhydryl groups, which helps transport mercury though the kidneys to be removed. All three suggestions should be taken at your highest comfortable dose.

---

[5]   Matsen (2002) *op. cit.* (note 2), pp. 7–8.

Neutralizing Peroxides

The health of your body is essentially determined by your liver's ability to neutralize toxins arriving from your gastrointestinal system. Your liver uses a two-step process involving phase one enzymes and phase two enzymes.

Your phase one enzymes add oxygen to fat-soluble chemicals called phenols. Oxygen molecules have two oxygen atoms. When one of the atoms gets added to the phenol, the other atom is left hanging without its buddy and becomes destructive to your body. You've probably heard of these destructive atoms as free radicals. Free radicals create peroxides, which is a natural and normal biochemical step, but if the peroxides aren't neutralized quickly by the phase two enzymes, they can cause a lot of damage, including digestive or bowel problems, urinary tract or skin issues, heart, joint or brain irritation and even immune or autoimmune reactions and cancer.

Glutathione peroxidase is one of the phase two enzymes that helps to neutralize peroxides. Unfortunately, the presence of mercury in the body can interrupt the natural process. The glutathione peroxidase enzyme needs sulfur and selenium to neutralize the peroxides, but since mercury binds to sulfur and displaces selenium, mercury drastically interferes with your liver's ability to do its job.

Heal Your Liver

- Avoid mercury in dental products, vaccines or amalgam fillings.
- Avoid alcohol, tobacco and coffee.
- Avoid refined sugar and flour, grains and table salt. Opt for sea salt instead.
- Eat food and herbs that supply your phase two enzymes with the nutrients they need: rye pollen, milk thistle herb, selenium (200 micrograms/day), whey protein powder, cruciferous vegetables, blue and purple foods such as blueberries or beets.
- If you have a chronic health problem, supplement with proanthocyanins such as grape seed extract or vitamin C with bioflavonoids.

Eliminate Intestinal Yeast

The main source of the phenols that your liver turns into peroxides is the yeast in your intestines. It's normal to have candida yeast in your intestinal tract (they turn you into compost when you die), but an overgrowth of them can cause health concerns. Maintaining a good pH balance in your large intestine with acidophilus bacteria will inhibit the growth.

Antibiotics, mercury, chlorinated water and antacids can inform the yeast to start composting while you're still alive! Once the yeasts are active, you may get intense cravings for sugar, especially at night! Dr. Matsen notes:

"Another way that the yeast can become active is when your ileocecal valve is weakened. The ileocecal valve is located between your small and your large intestine. This valve is usually kept closed so that the food you've eaten stays in your small intestine long enough to be digested and absorbed fully. It also prevents the good micro-organisms in your large intestine from getting into your small intestine, where its waste products could easily be absorbed. As digestion and absorption are completed in your small intestine, your ileocecal valve opens, and the food passes into your large intestine or colon.

When your ileocecal valve is weakened, the billions of normally good bacteria that live in the large intestine get through the ileocecal valve, up into your small intestine— where they're not supposed to be."[6]

When this happens, nutrients can be stolen before you have a chance to absorb them. The ileocecal valve can be weakened when calcium levels are low. Unfortunately, simply taking calcium supplements won't solve this dilemma, as it's vitamin D that is required for calcium to be absorbed.

When your skin is hit by the ultraviolet (UV) rays of the sun, it makes an inactive form of vitamin D that gets stored in your liver. When vitamin D is released, calcium absorption is activated. If you're out in the sun regularly, your skin has a chance to make a lot of vitamin D, which allows you to absorb calcium. Unfortunately, not all of us always get adequate sun.

Your kidneys use the food you eat to regulate their desired 50/50 ratio of potassium and sodium, eliminating excess sodium and potassium through the urine. When you eat lots of bananas for

---

6   Matsen (2002) *op. cit.* (note 2), p. 24.

example, you're telling your kidneys that you're getting adequate sunshine because you're in a tropical climate. Your kidneys will assume you're getting enough vitamin D (which is needed for calcium absorption) and tell your liver to stop converting it into a usable form to maintain balance. If you're actually in a cool climate with little sun, this could greatly weaken the ileocecal valve, which requires calcium to function properly.

To keep your ileocecal valve strong in cool climates, consume more sodium. If you eat meat regularly, you should get an adequate amount of sodium in your diet naturally. If you're a vegetarian, add sea salt to green vegetables. In warmer climates where your skin tans from the sun, you may elect to eat more fruits containing potassium.

Probiotics containing acidophilus bacteria can be purchased over-the-counter from your local pharmacy. Eat leafy green vegetables for vitamin K which your body requires to deliver calcium from your blood into your bones. Eat anti-inflammatory herbs such as basil, garlic, ginger, oregano, rosemary, turmeric and thyme.

Removing Toxic Grains from Your Diet

No living animal or plant wants to be consumed by humans. Fruit is an exception, desiring to be eaten so the seeds get excreted as waste. Animals have clever defense mechanisms for protection: claws, sharp fangs, poisonous skin and so on. Do plants also have ways to protect themselves from hungry predators? Yes, but because they don't view life from the same density as us, they've developed different strategies to propagate their species. The defense mechanisms in grains are what Mark Sisson, author of *The Primal Blueprint*, calls anti-nutrients. Certain animals, birds for example, are designed to consume grains with no difficulty. Humans, however, are not!

Anti-Nutrients Present in Grains

Sisson notes: "Lectins are bad. They bind to insulin receptors, attack the stomach lining of insects, bind to human intestinal lining, and they seemingly cause leptin resistance. Leptins are proteins produced by fatty tissues which regulate fat storage in the body. Leptin resistance creates a "worsening of the features of the metabolic syndrome independently of obesity"."[7]

Gluten-free diets have popped up all over the Western world, and for good reason. About 1% of the population are celiacs, people who are completely intolerant of gluten.

> "Twenty-nine percent of asymptomatic (read: not celiac) people nonetheless tested positive for anti-gliadin IgA in their stool. Anti-gliadin IgA is an antibody produced by the gut, and it remains there until it's dispatched to ward off gliadin—a primary component of gluten. Basically, the only reason anti-gliadin IgA ends up in your stool is because your body sensed an impending threat—gluten. If gluten poses no threat, the anti-gliadin IgA stays in your gut. And to think, most Americans eat this stuff on a daily basis."[8]

---

7   Mark Sisson, "Why Grains Are Unhealthy," last modified November 05, 2009, http://www.marksdailyapple.com/why-grains-are-unhealthy.

8   Sisson (2009): *op. cit.* (note 7)

Phytates are anti-nutrients which prevent your body from absorbing and using minerals.

What About Bread?

The bread we eat today isn't prepared the same way as the bread our grandparents once consumed. Sprouting or fermenting grains was a much more popular method that reduced anti-nutrients (like phytic acid) and made nutrients more available.

Katie Wells notes phytic acid is "a substance that reduces absorption of calcium, magnesium, iron, copper and zinc. This phytic acid is found in the bran of all grains, as well as the outer coating of seeds and nuts. Even after grains became more mainstream during the agricultural revolution, grains were allowed to sit in the fields for several weeks before threshing. This allowed the grains to be exposed to the elements and to sprout, which reduces the phytic acid content."[9]

Now, most of our bread is made with refined white flour that gets mixed with quick-rise commercial yeast. There is no reason why we should be eating it!

---

9   Katie Wells, "The Real Problem With Grains," last modified December 28, 2016, https://wellnessmama. com/575/problem-with-grains.

Tasty Alternatives:

The acronym BROWS can help you remember which grains contain gluten:

Barley

Rye

Oats

Wheat (includes kamut, einkorn and farro)

Spelt (a species of wheat)

Instead of destroying your intestinal lining and preventing your body from absorbing vital minerals, try out these alternatives:

- Opt for properly prepared whole grains that are soaked, fermented or sprouted. (This will help lower the phytic acid content.)
- Use quinoa or white rice instead of pasta.
- Use zucchini or squash in place of spaghetti.
- Use sweet potatoes in place of lasagna noodles.
- Use coconut or almond flour in place of refined wheat flour.

Sugar

The liver can only store 100 grams of glucose, and the muscles, 500 grams. When there is no more room left in the liver or muscles, glucose gets sent to your fat cells as a precautionary measure. If you overdo it on anything that breaks down into sugar in the body (bread, cakes, crackers, etc.), eventually your glucose receptors will resist the pressure of the pancreas to store anymore (the pancreas releases insulin to enable your insulin receptors to open so they can store glucose in the liver or fat cells.) When you consume an excess amount of sugar the pancreas has no choice but to release more insulin to get the sugar out of your blood stream and into your fat cells. When you continue to overeat sugar the glucose receptors become even more resistant to insulin and refuse to store anymore as fat, so the pancreas releases more insulin. Over time this can lead to type 2 diabetes, high blood pressure and metabolic syndrome.

Even though glucose levels can be extremely high, they may not be able to be used if your glucose receptors are resistant to insulin. This leads to cravings for more sugary foods for quick bursts of energy and the inability to lose weight. Switching to a high fat and protein diet may help return your insulin levels to normal, giving them a chance to rest and repair. Always consult a medical professional before changing your diet or health regime.

Sugar makes platelets (tiny blood cells that help your body form clots to stop bleeding) sticky, interferes with insulin function, damages teeth and feeds yeast, fungus and cancer cells. It lowers your immunity by interfering with vitamin C transport and can pull calcium and other vital minerals from the body.

Always avoid refined sugar. Cane sugar, agave or stevia are healthier alternatives. If you consume a meal with protein, wait at least three to five hours after your meal to eat sweets. When sweets and proteins are combined, your digestion is slower, allowing yeast and bacteria to become more active.

Meat

If you're going to consume meat, make sure to source out organic and grass-fed products. Before any meal, offer a prayer of thanks to Source:

"Dear Source, guides, angels, etc., thank you for this meal. Please take any of it (energetically) that you wish and bless it. Thank you, thank you, thank you."

You may choose to also thank the soul of the animal that you are consuming. Leaving a piece of your food out for the spirits as an offering at your altar, next to beautiful flowers or incense, is also appropriate. Prayers and offerings can remind you of how blessed you truly are and help keep you in a deep state of reverence and appreciation. The state of gratitude you put yourself in will make it much easier for you to actually receive the nutrients and qi of the food you're eating.

Note, however, that most meat contains trans fats, which are toxic and cannot be broken down by your body. A diet rich in living vegetables and plants is a much healthier option. Avoid processed meat altogether as it has been linked to developing cancer.

Water

A reverse osmosis filter can remove fluoride, lead, chlorine and chloramine, pesticides, detergents, nitrates and sulphates from your water. Consider investing in a filter for your home and always check water bottle labels for fluoride. Never consume water with fluoride, ever!

Talking to your water or infusing it with crystals can be a powerful way to boost your mood and overall health. You can try this out for yourself by adding a piece of quartz to a glass of filtered water. Quartz works to amplify healing energy. Before you drink the water, command the quartz to heal, energize and strengthen you. Give the quartz a moment to communicate to the water. Take in a few slow, deep breaths to prepare your body for the healing. Drink the water and store the crystal anywhere you like for later use.

Healthy and Unhealthy Fats

Some fats promote cancer and heart disease and make you fat, tired and greasy. Others inhibit cancer and heart disease and keep you thin, energized and glowing. Which ones are which?

While high-fat diets can be healthy for you, consuming too many hard fats, found in animal and dairy products, can lead to health concerns. Since we live a more sedentary lifestyle now, a lot of us at the computer all day, we don't have the ability to burn off hard fats like we used to. An excess of these types of fats makes platelets sticky and interferes with insulin function and essential fatty acids. Platelets are cell fragments with no nucleus, which are involved in blood clotting. If sticky, they can form together and cause unwanted blood clots.

On the other hand, consuming diets with little or no fats can be equally as harmful! Usually the products marketed to you as low-fat are loaded with sugar or chemicals to compensate for their lack of flavour. They are food-like products, but not real food!

During the hydrogenation of fats, essential fatty acids are turned into molecules called trans-fatty acids that don't normally exist in nature. Stay away from margarines, shortenings or partially hydrogenated oils (trans fats) entirely. Hydrogenated fats have been shown to cause cardiovascular disease, lower the good cholesterol (HDL) and increase the bad (LDL).

Saturated fats are a stable fat source found mainly in dairy products and meat. Each molecule is covered in hydrogen atoms. Coconuts, egg yolks, cashews, salmon and dark chocolate are some great examples. Don't overdo it on the meat or dairy products, as they usually contain trans fats.

Unsaturated fats are a less stable fat source as they contain fewer hydrogen molecules, their chemical structure being quite complex and prone to alteration when exposed to heat. Avoid cooking with unsaturated fats and leaving them out for too long after using them. This can turn them rancid and toxic to your body. Sources of monounsaturated fats are avocados, olive oil, canola oil, grape seed oil, almond oil, sesame oil and sunflower seed oil.

Frying fats chemically changes their molecules. When you consume fried fats, your body can't possess the altered molecules. Along with stress, diseases such as cancer may arise from an overexposure to these altered molecules. Instead of frying with oils, stick to steaming your vegetables with water!

Out of the 50 essential nutrients your body needs to function, two of them are found in fat: the essential fatty acids, also known as polyunsaturated fats. You know them as omega-three (alpha-linoleic acid) and omega-six (linoleic acid). The essential fatty acids increase your energy, metabolic rate and help your kidneys dump excess water. They also elevate your mood, satisfy cravings, inhibit tumour growth, treat fungus and help strengthen your skin, hair and nails.

Your brain is mostly made of fat, the ratio of omega-three-to-six inside being 1:1. Aiming for a ratio of 2.5:1 will make it easy for your body to take what it needs to function optimally. A 3:1 ratio is even better.

Foods rich in omega-three are: flax seed oil, salmon, avocado, dark green leafy vegetables, hemp oil, chia seed, seaweed, flaxseed oil, perilla, sacha inchi seeds, oysters, soybeans (roasted).

Foods rich in omega-six are: hemp oil, soybean oil, corn oil, sunflower oil, safflower oil, pine nuts.

Superfoods

Superfoods are jam-packed with vitamins, protein, good fats and antioxidants. They provide you with all your essential nutrients while boosting your immunity, energizing your body, enhancing your mood, and cleansing and alkalizing your system. As they work to provide you with proper nutrition, they actually help maintain the homeostasis of your body, keeping your mood and energy levels balanced.

The most amazing part is that you'll never have to worry about overeating! Superfoods are rich, tasty and completely satisfying! It's nearly impossible to gain weight when you're eating such clean healthy food. Once you start eating superfoods, you'll start to feel so good that you won't ever want to go back to eating processed foods with empty calories. You'll start to fall in love with your food, which means you'll fall in love with your body and fall in love with life! Eating superfoods is not just a short-term fix. It's a diet that will literally change your entire life. Superfoods not only allow you to live a happier life, but a healthier and longer life.

Superfoods that you can start incorporating into your diet include cacao, maca, quinoa, spirulina, matcha, coconut, goji berries and hemp. Almost all of the superfoods listed are complete proteins, which means they have at least nine essential amino acids, from which they can create all 22 that we require!

Increasing Your Oxygen Intake

Negative ions (the good ones) are commonly found near mountains, waterfalls and oceans. No wonder these are often vacation spots! Fresh air also contains positive and negative ions that affect hormones such as serotonin. The daily movements of the sun and moon, the changes in weather patterns and the presence of plants and water can all create fluctuations in ion levels.

The air in sealed office buildings with air-conditioning, as you may imagine, is lacking in negative ions, which leads to poor health, stress, depression and increased susceptibility to infections.

You can increase your intake of negative ions by:

- Keeping a negative ion generator at your home or office. You may elect to purchase a cheaper, portable generator that you can clip directly onto your clothing.
- Keeping a salt lamp in your home or office.
- Filling your home with plants.
- Leaving at least one window open at all times, even at night.
- Going for regular walks in nature, especially near rushing water or high-altitude places with lots of natural vegetation.

Getting a Good Night's Rest

Going to bed and getting at least six to eight hours of sleep each night as an adult is essential for optimal health. Your circadian rhythms, intimately affected by the seasons, tell your body to sleep at night and rise in the morning. When you ignore these rhythms, your hormones are also affected.

When you stay up late with the lights on in front of a bright screen watching your favourite films, you can trick your body into thinking it's summer, even in the dead of winter. To compensate, your body will begin to crave carbohydrates to fuel you, so you can stay awake longer.

Cortisol, the stress hormone, also gets released when you regularly stay up late, to give you an extra boost of energy. This causes your insulin levels to rise to store sugar as fat. We all know what happens when too much insulin is released over time: insulin resistance and type 2 diabetes.

The answer? Aim to sleep before 10:00 p.m. Some natural sleep remedies are:

- Valerian
- Passionflower
- Ashwagandha
- Magnolia bark
- California poppy
- Lavender

Most of the herbs listed above can be consumed as teas before bed.

Melatonin should be used with caution, or not used at all, as the side effects can include daytime drowsiness, headaches, inability to fall asleep without Melatonin, dizziness, stomach cramps and irritability.

Keep a Dream Journal

Once you start going to bed at a reasonable hour your body will thank you! You may be surprised to find that your dreams become much more vivid and memorable. Keep a dream journal next to your bed and as soon as you wake up in the morning, try not to move. Then write down as many details as you can from your dream: sights, sounds, tastes, time of day, etc. Tracing your way from the end of your dream back to the start is usually easier than going the opposite route. With practice, recalling your dreams becomes second nature. Look back at your dream journal every month or so. What recurring patterns do you see? What messages is you higher self sharing with you? Have any spirit guides presented themselves to you?

Hypnopompic and Hypnagogic

Just as you're about to fall asleep you enter into a hypnagogic state. As you're waking, still in between worlds, you're in the hypnopompic state. These states are a great time to take a jab at automatic writing. Often during these states, we channel our higher self and amazing pearls of wisdom come through.

To try this out for yourself, prepare for your channelling session before bed by setting your journal and pen within reach of where you sleep. Set an intention to channel your higher self or any guides or angels you wish to work with. If you want to place a particular crystal next to your journal or under your pillow, feel free to do so. Labradorite or kunzite are great crystals to use as they help safely awaken psychic gifts. Placing a piece of clear quartz or selenium next to your journal or underneath your pillow will keep your energetic field pure and safe from any psychic attacks. Make sure you're really tired for this exercise, already on the verge of sleep. Set an alarm for 20 minutes. Lie down and allow yourself to completely relax. When the alarm rings, quickly grab your pen and begin writing without pause. Allow any thoughts to pour out of you without restraint or editing.

If you're lucky enough to realize that you're in the hypnopompic state upon waking, grab your pen and begin to write without stopping. Over time, these practices will get easier. Just as you can look over your dream journal for messages or themes from spirit, you can look over your channelled messages for inspiration and guidance.

Setting an Intention Before Bed

It's a great idea to set an intention before bed. Do you want to meet your spirit guide or visit a loved one? Simply command yourself to do so as you lie in bed.

You can also choose to write down a command on a piece of paper and place it with a crystal under your pillow. Alternatively, you can leave the command on your bedside table and place the crystal on it. To activate it, draw three clockwise circles around the command and say aloud: "Dear Source, I love you and appreciate you with all my soul. As an aspect of God, I command you to activate this intention through me, and so it is." Add in whatever other affirmations or spells feel right. Your natural magic is more powerful when it's in alignment with your heart!

Performing a Full Organ Cleanse Can:

- Balance your hormones.
- Provide you with relief from digestive problems and inflammation.
- Release stress.
- Restore bacteria balance to improve immunity and rid the body of excess estrogen.
- Restore proper communication from the nervous system to the brain to control appetite and improve metabolism.
- Rid the body of toxins, fat and hormonal waste.
- Help the body absorb nutrients more effectively.
- Eliminate waste more effectively.
- Alleviate skin issues.
- Cause your skin and hair to glow.
- Make you feel fantastic!

There are five steps to an organ cleanse. It's important to cleanse the organs in order so toxins won't spill into other organs. The order is as follows:

- Kidneys
- Colon
- Liver and gallbladder
- Small intestine
- Blood

Cleanse the Kidneys

The kidneys are bean-shaped organs the size of a fist that sit just below your ribs on each side of the spine. They filter 120-150 quarts of blood/day to produce one to two quarts of urine. They prevent the buildup of wastes and extra fluids within the body. They keep electrolytes such as potassium, sodium and phosphate stable. They make hormones that regulate blood pressure, make red blood cells and keep bones strong.

Drink lots of water containing no fluoride. Four litres per day is ideal. Get a big water bottle and bring it with you everywhere. Keep track of how much you're drinking. Four litres seems like a lot, but it's actually rather do-able. If you want to make the water tastier, add in some lemon wedges. Lemons will help stimulate your liver's bile production to remove toxins.

Drink pure, unsweetened cranberry juice. One big glass a day will do. Cranberries are anti-bacterial and contain proanthocyanidins which prevent free-radical damage.

To strengthen the kidneys, cultivate wisdom. The kidneys, along with the lungs, are the organs that stimulate your jing energy, your sexual energy. Jing energy keeps your bones healthy and strong. It creates bone marrow and the grey matter of your brain.

Cleanse the Colon

The colon, or large intestine, absorbs water and minerals and forms and eliminates feces. It contains microflora to help with digestion and nutrient production, preventing harmful bacteria from growing.

Invest in a natural colon cleanse product. A website I trust and recommend with 100% integrity is www.enerhealthbontanicals.com.

Ingredients usually found in a colon cleanse product include:

Organic cinnamon: alleviates fungal infections, balances blood sugar, is anti-bacterial, prevents cancer and Alzheimer's, is a mood enhancer.

Whole and ground chia: is high in protein, contains all nine essential amino acids, is a natural energizer.

Organic marshmallow root: is anti-bacterial, soothes the throat, produces a sticky substance that coats membranes (mucilage), contains flavonoids, which have anti-inflammatory properties. The flavonoids reduce inflammation while the mucilage holds them in place and prevents further damage. Marshmallow extract also induces phagocytosis, which allows cells to engulf bacteria and dead cell tissues or other solid particles, speeding up the healing process.

Organic psyllium hulls: are a good source of fibre, reduce appetite, improve digestion, cleanse your system.

Human grade bentonite: absorbs toxins in the colon and helps safely remove them. Bentonite clays originate from volcanic ash deposits that over thousands-to-millions of years turn into clay minerals.

Apple pectin: balances blood sugar levels, prevents colon cancer, provides a chelating effect (urinary excretion of heavy metals), speeds excretion of toxins from the body.

Organic ginger: aids in digestion, contains chromium, magnesium and zinc, improves immunity, nutrition absorption and blood flow, prevents colon cancer, reduces pain and inflammation. Ginger is a natural expectorant and clears mucus out of the lungs, bronchi and trachea.

Activated charcoal: reduces the body's absorption of poisonous substances by up to 60%, absorbs chemicals through the digestive tract and reduces their toxicity.

Mix one teaspoon of your colon cleanse mix with a big glass of filtered, non-fluorinated water. Repeat up to four times daily. Cleansing the colon may make you constipated. If you use a product that contains human grade bentonite, the toxins and waste material that have collected in your colon will stick to the clay to be purged from your body. This can be slightly uncomfortable at first. If you decide to cleanse with clay, it's a good idea to invest in a laxative as well.

Cleanse the Liver and Gallbladder

The liver is a large, meaty organ that sits on the right side of your belly. It screens the blood for toxins, viruses and bacteria. It detoxifies alcohol and drugs and plays a major role in how strong our immune system is. It creates bile used to break down fats and remove toxins.

Bile is stored in the gallbladder, a small organ that sits just beneath the liver. The liver and gallbladder can become overwhelmed by large amounts of processed foods, grains, alcohol and toxins.

To cleanse both these organs, you can complete an Epsom salt cleanse that will require two days of your time. To begin the cleanse, you want to make sure that you're okay to consume Epsom salts. Consult your doctor before you begin any cleanse and do not perform an Epsom salt cleanse if you are pregnant.

Epsom salt (magnesium sulfate) is a naturally occurring mineral comprised of oxygen, hydrogen, sulfur and magnesium. Consuming it creates a laxative effect by relaxing the digestive muscles. If you experience a lack of muscle control, nausea or blushing, consult a medical professional. If you want to enjoy the healing, detoxifying benefits of Epsom salts, but do not want to consume them, you can always take a bath with two cups of the salts. Soaking in the salts will help ease your muscles and draw out toxins from your skin.

The magnesium in Epsom salts is especially important. Almost all enzymatic functions within the body require the presence of magnesium. It's involved in energy production, protein formation, cell replication and muscle relaxation. Magnesium is essential for converting sugar to ATP, the fuel for human cells.

In plant life, magnesium acts like a magnet to bind oxygen to the living cells of the plant. Without the plant blood that is magnesium, there would be no plant life and without plant life, we wouldn't be able to exist on Earth!

What You Will Need for an Epsom Salt Cleanse

- Two completely free days
- Three cups apple juice
- Four tablespoons Epsom salts
- One-half cup virgin olive oil
- Three lemons

Instructions:

To prepare for the Epsom salt cleanse, eat lots of apples or drink lots of apple juice a few days leading up to the cleanse. Apples contain malic acid, which helps to open up the bile duct that runs through your liver. Instead of drinking apple juice or eating apples, you can also choose to consume malic acid supplements.

On the day of the cleanse, eat a breakfast that contains no fat. Fruits and veggies are a good idea. This will enable the bile in the liver to accumulate, putting pressure on your liver. Pressure will help eliminate any stones.

At 2:00 p.m., stop consuming any food. Mix four tablespoons of Epsom salts in three cups of apple juice. Put the mixture in a glass jar and store it in the fridge to cool.

At 6:00 p.m., drink a three-quarter cup dose of your Epsom salt mixture (there will be four doses in total).

At 8:00 p.m., drink a second three-quarter cup dose. Get all your chores done and relax.

At 9:45 p.m., pour a one-half cup of virgin olive oil into a separate glass jar. Squeeze in the juice of three lemons. Shake until mixed thoroughly.

At 10:00 p.m., drink the olive oil and lemon mixture. Get it down within five minutes.

Lie down as soon as you finish the mixture and go to sleep. Lay on your right side with your knees pulled up to your chin.

At 8:00 a.m. the next morning, drink another three-quarter cup of the Epsom salt mixture. Go back to bed.

At 10:00 a.m., drink the last Epsom salt dose.

By noon, you can resume eating. Start with fruit juice and work your way up to solid fruits. Then start adding in healthy fats. Avocados work well.

Epsom salts are a natural laxative. Expect to spend a lot of time on the toilet if you decide to go through with this cleanse. Also expect to feel rejuvenated, renewed and invigorated when it's all over! Do not consume Epsom salts for longer than one week.

Cleanse the Small Intestine

The small intestine absorbs nutrients in food that are broken down in the stomach. Acid and mucus heavy diets cause excess mucus (called mucoid) to line the small intestine and interfere with absorption of nutrients into the bloodstream. Small intestine cleansing removes the mucoid.

Consume bromelain, a digestive enzyme that is derived from the stems of pineapples that can be taken as a supplement. It's also found in the fruit of the pineapples as well. Eat your pineapples to help cleanse the small intestine!

Consume papain, a cysteine protease enzyme found in papayas. Cysteine protease enzymes are enzymes that degrade proteins.

Drink mullein leaf tea. The proteins caught in the mucoid lining must be removed for mucus-removing mullein to be able to remove mucus. Mullein is a weed that grows in Europe, N. Africa, Asia, America and Australia. It treats respiratory conditions, skin conditions and urinary tract infections. The leaves are rich in magnesium and iron. Mullein can be found in health food stores.

To make mullein tea, pour one cup of boiling water over one to two teaspoons of dried mullein. Cover and steep for 10-15 minutes. Pour the liquid through a coffee filter or cheesecloth to strain out any of the plant hairs, which can irritate the throat. Drink up to three cups per day and sweeten with raw sugar if you desire.

Slippery elm is another herb to consume while cleansing and repairing the small intestine. When combined with water, slippery elm creates a jelly-like coating on the internal linings of the digestive tract. This prevents leaky gut syndrome and soothes irritation.

Cleanse the Blood

Blood is a combination of plasma (a watery liquid) and the cells that float in it. It supplies essential substances and nutrients such as sugar, oxygen and hormones to your cells. It carries waste from those cells, which is eventually flushed from the body through urination, feces, sweat and breathing.

A blood cleansing tea is a great way to purify the blood safely. Herbs to consume are as follows:

Red clover blossom: soothes coughs and colds, eases asthma, calms skin irritations, treats anxiety and insomnia.

Chaparral leaf: treats arthritis, bowel cramps, skin conditions, stomach problems, PMS, gallbladder issues, kidney stones and respiratory conditions.

Echinacea root: treats colds and boosts immunity.

Yellow dock root: purifies and detoxifies blood, stimulates bile production which helps in digestion of fats, stimulates bowels and urination to help eliminate toxins.

Violet leaves: contains antioxidants, vitamin C, and bioflavonoids such as rutin, loaded with carotenes, helps with bowel movements, heals gastrointestinal tract, eases headaches, treats bronchitis, is anti-inflammatory and antiseptic. The chemical compound saponins gives violet the ability to dissolve cysts, tumors and nodules, especially in breasts.

Uva ursi leaves: treat the bladder and remove toxins from the kidneys, contain arbutin which has an antiseptic effect on urinary tract infections.

Other Noteworthy Herbs, Plants and Algae to Add to Your Cleanse

Dandelion: is a diuretic that purifies blood, dissolves kidney stones, improves GI tract health, assists in weight reduction, alleviates skin problems, improves bowel function, lowers blood pressure, prevents cancer.

Burdock root: is a natural diuretic, helps remove toxins, balances blood sugar, is anti-bacterial and anti-inflammatory, treats skin issues.

Sarsaparilla: is anti-inflammatory and anti-bacterial, is a diuretic, flushes kidneys, improves sexual desire.

Milk thistle: detoxifies the liver, lowers cholesterol, reduces growth of cancer cells in the breast, lung, colon, prostate, cervix and kidney; improves blood sugar levels, has anti-aging properties, is a powerful antioxidant, helps with GI tract issues.

Chlorella: is powerful antioxidant, binds to heavy metals and helps to remove them, contains B12.

Spirulina: is powerful antioxidant, contains B12, energizes the body.

Cilantro: binds to heavy metals and removes them from the body.

Garlic: is a powerful anti-fungal and is important for cleansing the body.

Gotu kola: is an ayurvedic herb which improves memory and cognitive functioning, treats chronic skin conditions, fever, venereal diseases, helps with respiratory congestion, strengthens immunity, strengthens the adrenals, cleanses the blood, improves nervous conditions, helps with insomnia.

Cat's Claw: creates support for intestinal and immune system, is anti-inflammatory and anti-cancer. Helps those with stomach difficulties and bowel disorders including: Crohn's disease, irritable bowel syndrome and leaky bowel syndrome.

PART 3

Heal Mental Blockages

Staying Aware

When you spend the majority of your time in your head, thinking about what you have to do in a future moment, or perhaps reminiscing about the past, this may feel like an intense aliveness. Thinking is often associated with intelligence, but the mind is simply a tool and one that we've been misusing for far too long. When you live in the mind solely, this cuts you off from your body, from your true essence. It's not that thinking is bad or wrong. In fact, thinking is an automatic function that you cannot shut off, but when you start to identify with your thoughts and start to view your judgments about yourself as truths about who you really are, this always results in suffering. The same goes for projections cast onto other people, events, circumstances or things.

The mind is a master problem solver, but as with everything in this dualistic world, it's also a problem generator. When you view the world only from your mind, attaching to the labels you give yourself to create an identity, inevitably there will always be something wrong for you to focus on. The ego in particular—your sense of individuated self—will always seek to separate itself from the world around you in order to protect itself. The insatiable and highly unstable ego fears its own death, and thus attacks other egos to build itself up so it can stay alive and sovereign.

Identifying with the story your ego constantly loves to invent in order to preserve itself actually puts you into a state of deep unconsciousness. When you choose to feed the mind incessantly by attaching to any passing thought, you create blockages within your energetic body that make it difficult for your vital energy to flow freely. This may seem to create a sense of power or control, but in truth, only keeps you stuck in a state of separation, disconnected from your true power which must always be witnessed with your consciousness, not through the veil of thought. When looking at the world through the lens of the ego, you will never see the greater truth that all is one.

Thoughts are simply that—thoughts. Sometimes they are passing judgments about our external reality that serve no other purpose than to protect the physical body. As receivers of light and information from Source consciousness, it is our duty to learn how to master the mind, to learn to use it as a tool to receive higher dimensional information; to bring the light of God into this world and create heaven on Earth now.

As you walk down the street, become intensely aware of your feet hitting the ground beneath you. Breathe into your form and send your awareness deep into your body. Can you feel the aliveness in your legs, the power carrying you forward? Maintain a constant awareness of the aliveness within your body as you go about your day. This will enable you to stay grounded and conscious. If you catch yourself craving the need to feed the often societally engrained addiction to thinking, simply focus on your breath. Slow down and send your awareness back into the depths of your being. Breathe into your root chakra to return to a state of presence, the state of calm alertness that is your natural way of being.

Allow yourself to witness without thinking. Simply observe the world around you. If you feel the need to start labelling things as good or bad, return to the breath. Can you observe without thought? If fear arises at first when you begin to let go of the need to think, breathe into the uncomfortable sensation. Invite the fear to observe with you. Continue to breathe, witness and ask, "Who is witnessing this reality? Who sees from these eyes? Who thinks with this brain? Who feels with this heart? Who moves with this form? Who is being breathed into life?"

When you talk about your problems to a friend, notice that you use the word *I*. Question, "Who is I?" Who really is the *I* that you speak about? Most often we tend to identify with our thoughts about ourselves, but not our true selves. When we look at the world from the mind alone, thinking that we are that mind, we look at the world through limitation and lack. We identify with something that doesn't even truly exist: our imagined sense of identity, a personality we've dreamed into existence. But not us, not the real us, the eternal us that knows no fear.

In order for this information to truly sink in, it must be witnessed through the simple act of observation in the present moment. What is going on within you? What is going on without? Can you observe both without thinking? If we think even for a moment that we are our bodies, brains or emotions, we are living a lie. You are free to indulge in any of your senses or lose yourself in your emotions to feel a sense of aliveness, but focusing solely on your thoughts, for example, is akin to painting a masterpiece with only one colour.

When we approach life from the lens of our true self, the lens of the soul, we can no longer be hurt. The only time you can truly be hurt is when you identify with your imaginary self, the ego. It's only the ego that fears its own death, not you. You, in your true form, which is formless and timeless—the spaciousness within you that will never die—do not fear if the holographic projection in front of your eyes changes. In fact, it loves change and often invites it. Your soul decided to come to Earth for the excitement and learning that comes with change.

This part of you is already complete and always has been complete. When this knowledge is felt in its entirety, fear can exist within you as a safety mechanism, but it can no longer hurt you. You see that fear itself is also an illusion you've created for a sense-of-self and that when you face that fear, it no longer has any power over you. Fear only becomes detrimental when you run from it by remaining locked within the confines of the mind, by worrying about fear itself! Any tension can only exist when it's fed with thought. When thoughts cease, so does the tension.

When you're in the state of presence, fully aware that you are in fact a divine being that is already perfect, with no need to do or become anything, you're set free. It becomes instantly clear that when others say, "I'm not good enough," they've only forgotten who they truly are. Their divine selves would not say that, because it would be a lie. Only one identified with the mind can imagine that they are anything less than divine!

The question remains, why are we imagining ourselves to be so small, so limited and so worthless, when in fact we are divine aspects of God? A simple observation of the world we live in will point to the dysfunctional system we, as a collective, have dreamed into existence. The external world, a reflection of the world within, shows us that we have been giving our power away for thousands of years now. While we can blame the news, the government, the educational intuitions, etc., for our problems, to do so would only enforce the outdated victim consciousness we no longer need to subscribe to. It's time now to rise up out of the brainwashing of the media and reclaim our power as divine beings incarnate in human form. It's time to learn how to use that power to heal ourselves and create a better world. We all have the power to choose to let go of our past and start anew right now.

That choice is as simple as staying present and offering love to yourself and everyone you meet. No matter what arises, offer the same love, the highest love from Source consciousness. Doing this will heal this world and allow you to once again walk this Earth free from the bondage of the lower mind, enslaved to a physical world and to your physical form!

Ancient knowledge has been purposely hidden from us to keep us enslaved to our base instincts and emotions. Our education systems prepare us for life; they train us how to be subservient slaves to a system that only serves the government and the corporations that fund it. We have doctors for the body and psychiatrists for the brain but, at least in the Western world, we've ignored the soul. It's this vital part of the human experience that we've lost our connection to that is causing so much suffering.

Our water has been poisoned with fluoride, and our food with pesticides and other harmful chemicals. Why? So the people who claim to run this world can continue to profit off our ignorance so we remain enslaved to a system that only benefits them.

This is done mostly through the monetary system. If you didn't have to pay for energy that could be free and food that could also be free, would you really have to spend eight hours a day slaving away at an unsatisfying job? I know I wouldn't! It's never been money itself that's brought about beautiful technologies that have propelled us into the next evolutionary phase of existence. It's always been humans coming together to create. This is where our power lies. We are creative beings who have the ability to tap into our limitless potential, to think, act and manifest from our highest divine authority to change this world. It's our imagination, our innate magic that terrifies the ones who want to keep the world asleep. Have you ever wondered why media works so hard to make you afraid, to make you feel small and incomplete? The word government translates to mind control and that's what been occurring for far too long on Earth. The distortion of our perception is mostly done through brainwashing and subliminal programming through the use of symbols in the media, along with the indoctrination that is our supposed education. The people in power know that if you choose to wake up to who you truly are, they will no longer be able to rule and oppress as they've been doing for thousands of years.

Think about it logically. If you were to fully realize your divine nature and limitless potential for creation, would you really feel the need to buy 20 pairs of shoes to feel more whole? Of course not! The entire money system will collapse when we all decide to step into our true power together.

It's not that money is evil. It's a neutral energy that people have been using to control others. Before we switch to a new system where money may or may not exist, we have to harmonize with it and not view it as evil. Seeing money as something evil will only give it more power to affect your life negatively. Currency is literally a current of energy that reflects the abundance you feel within, along with the service you offer the world. It's a symbol we're collectively choosing to give meaning to. We've used all sorts of symbols for money in the past, including sea shells and cacao beans!

Instead of wasting your energy being angry at money itself, which is neutral, take back your power by becoming present. Watch where you're placing your attention. It's true that where attention goes, energy flows. If you think of yourself like a mirror, receiving the same frequencies you choose to emit, why not choose to focus on the abundance all around you? No matter how hard your situation may be to endure, if you have access to clean water, healthy food and fresh air, you're amazingly abundant compared to almost half the population of the world. Can you look around you right now and list 10 things that you're grateful to have? It's the vibration of gratitude that brings us everything we desire. The funny thing is that when we create this vibration, we see that we no longer need anything to feel safe or whole.

From a higher perspective, we realize that even the evil we feel we have to fight against is just a distortion of love that will inevitably return to the exact same Source we all will. The ascent of the soul is inevitable. Realizing this, it's clear to see that we chose to have the evils of this world to fight against for fun. In reality, however, there never was, never will be and never is any evil. All is love. All is one.

What's the Point of it All?

If you do decide to step out of victim mentality and fully grasp on all levels that you are one with everything, suddenly there is nothing that needs to happen. You no longer need to fill your life with clothes, food, friends, or objects to feel safe or secure. You deeply feel that you already are that which you seek. So then, what's the point of coming here if you're already complete?

To play!

As a divine being with limitless power to create, you chose to come to Earth to enjoy, to laugh, to explore this realm! What a relief to know that you're already perfect! What a relief to know that nothing needs to get done in order for you to be worthy of love, respect, peace and utter bliss!

What a relief to know that you are not the story you tell about yourself and if you deviate from that story, nothing wrong or bad will ever happen. Nothing bad can ever happen because this is all just play. Even if you do something that offends someone else or triggers them, you're only offending their story, their idea of who they are, which doesn't even exist! This knowledge doesn't give you permission to hurt others. Indeed, if you are centred in being, you see that all is one and the desire to hurt another doesn't arise. We only attack others when we're mind-identified.

When you choose to stop controlling life or manipulating others to fit into your story of how things should go, you give life a chance to teach you. You give God a chance to manifest miracles through you.

Think back to a time in your life where you've been intensely frustrated. I know I tend to be a little bit of a space cadet when it comes to misplacing very useful objects such as my keys! Once after searching for hours on end for them, complaining all the while of course, I got so frustrated that I just gave up searching and decided to read a book. While I was reading and relaxing, the vision of my keys sitting on my kitchen counter suddenly hit me. I started laughing and thought, why couldn't I see them before? Sound familiar?

Life always gives you exactly what you need, not what your mind wants. Whether the mind can comprehend this or not, what you receive is always for your highest benefit, for the growth of your soul. When you rush through life with an overstimulated nervous system, constantly thinking, you cut yourself off from the flow of energy that wants to move miracles through you. Even your frustration arises to lead you back to your true self, which is always peaceful, loving and compassionate.

Today I invite you to make the choice to stop resisting life as if it's out to get you. Life doesn't have to be a burden if you choose to change your perspective. When you view the universe as kind and look through the eyes of your higher self, you see that all is unfolding exactly as planned. When you send love to the moment you're in, whatever that moment may be, life turns into a beautiful gift, a playground for you to frolic in.

When you rise above the lower mind and step into your divine authority, faith becomes your way of being and you move through life gracefully, knowing that you've always been and you always will be protected by the divine. Only the mind can lie to you otherwise, but if you turn within and sit with your own being, soon you'll see that you've never been the person you've imagined yourself to be.

You've always been whole and completely free.

<hr>

Staying Present

The practice of presence is an art form that does require effort—the effort being your vigilance and dedication to staying fully alert in the moment. With time and practice it does get easier to realize when you've drifted back into unconsciousness. One of the simplest ways to stay aware is to become deeply intimate with your body.

When you exist within the mind alone, thinking constantly, you become like a mind alone walking through life, disconnected from your body. You begin to lose touch with what your body is trying to communicate to you. Are you aware of the messages your heart yearns to share? Can you feel the subtle contractions within your form, warning you of danger?

If not, you must become reacquainted. Spend some time in silence observing your body. Scan each part of your form from head to toe. If you sense any discomfort in a particular area, question it: "What are you telling me?" The body often uses physical or emotional pain to warn us when we're falling too far into unconsciousness. A back ache may signify that you don't feel supported. A sore wrist may be a sign that you don't have a grasp on your life. When you exist in the mind alone, attaching to every passing thought, you can convince yourself that you're healthy when in reality you're hurting yourself.

Have you ever had to work overtime at a job you didn't like? Perhaps your body told you that it was time to rest, but your mind insisted that you had to stay at work to make money. This kind of behaviour is so common in the Western world that we laugh it off like it's just natural or a part of life, when in fact it's toxic. The accompanying stress creates sickness within the body, which in some cases is literally killing us. When the energy of the mind is stagnant from too much thinking, the rest of the energy in the body cannot flow properly. Energy blockages, especially negative thought forms or emotions, can eventually manifest into emotional or physical dis-ease.

Have you ever eaten even though you were already sated? Why did you do it? Were you listening to the demands of your mind telling you that you deserved something sweet? It's a choice to feed the ego or to step back into presence. Listen to your body and choose health.

Even our accidents are never really accidents, but instead are always there to help us return to a state of presence. Have you ever been mad at yourself and stubbed your toe? Did the pain wake you up and instantly take you out of your head? Could that possibly have been a message from spirit redirecting you back to your centre?

It's not that thinking is wrong. It's simply a tool that you can learn to use while conscious. If you do decide to venture into the past to revisit a happy memory, do so with awareness. As you drift back into the memory, make sure you're breathing slowly and comfortably. As you think, maintain the awareness that you are indeed thinking. As you think, place some of your attention on your inner energy. If you catch your energy starting to concentrate in the mind alone, if you lose your connection to your body, take in a deep breath and sink back down into your form. Your thoughts should never take you away from your being.

Balancing the Brain Hemispheres

If you identify as a creative person, someone with a lot of right brain activity, it's likely that sitting down and simply listening to a motivational speaker to change the way you think isn't going to cut it for you. You'll most likely need to occupy the right hemisphere of the neo-cortex (the part of the brain associated with hearing and sight in mammals) to allow the left hemisphere to concentrate on taking in new information, especially logical information, such as language.

If you find yourself in a situation that doesn't capture your attention such as listening to a boring lecture, it's likely that you'll start to daydream. The act of doodling may serve to stop you from daydreaming and help keep you focused on the task at hand.

I remember back in a college psychology lecture, when my professor would speak, I would inevitably start to drift off, and the only way I could maintain full focus was to start doodling to feed my right brain. As I drew absentmindedly, scribbling mandalas alongside my notes, I noticed I was then able to actually absorb and remember the words I was hearing. This is of course contrary to the outdated suggestion of sit still and be quiet!

You are a Creator

Often when we feel like we're stuck in a rut, we go to the brain to solve our problems. Unfortunately, it's usually our attachment to thinking that creates the problems in the first place! The solution is of course to get out of your head and into your heart! One of the easiest ways to reconnect to your heart is through creating art.

If you're a more left-brained person, the idea of sitting down to even start on your masterpiece can seem a little daunting, but I'm here to remind you that we are *all* creative beings with a unique message to share.

Art as a Spiritual Practice

Think back to when you were a child. What sort of activities were you naturally drawn to? Did you like to paint, write, put on plays, dance or sing? As a child, you were intimately connected to your heart, to Source consciousness. You didn't have to think about what you wanted to create. You just did it! Can you remember the feeling that arose within you as a child while you danced and laughed uninhibitedly?

It's this feeling that, unfortunately more often than not, we try to re-create through incessant thinking, which only brings fleeting flashes of pleasure and often more confusion. These flashes are nothing compared to the bliss that can only be felt with a return to presence.

Pause for a moment to reflect on your current desires. Why do you really want what you want? If you dig deep enough, you'll see that anything you desire, whether a person, object or experience, you crave to create positive emotions. Feelings of safety, of peace and of love.

Through the act of creating art you surrender to the force of love that wants to move through you into this world. You don't have to think about how you're one with everything; you can feel it with every fibre of your being. Suddenly there is no more yearning for the light. You see that you are the light of God manifesting this reality in every moment. Your entire life and everything you witness becomes your creation. You are the creator.

Spiritual activities that we perform such as yoga or Qigong help us to clear our energetic channels so we can live in a state of perfect harmony, in flow with the will of the divine, dancing through life effortlessly and gracefully. In the same respect, art can be treated as a spiritual practice that allows you to transcend the mundane and enter deeply into the moment, where you can connect with your higher self, your angels, spirit team and animal guides.

If you've spent time in meditation, you know how beneficial it is to shut off the brain momentarily. When you think, you actually send off random thought forms into the world and sometimes unconsciously create unnecessary drama for yourself, especially if you never take the time to witness those thought forms.

Through surrendering to a creative practice that allows you to step into your intuition, you give yourself a mental break and at the same time begin to channel healing spiritual energy. Let me explain what happens when I paint:

> The less I think about what I'm painting, the better I perform. If I succumb to the force of love that wants to pour forth from my heart through my fingertips, I see how easily my hand dances across my canvas. I rely on my enteric system for simple movements, such as dipping my brush in water and fully allow myself to be taken by the colours I'm seeing. With music to accompany the movements, the creative act soon becomes a magic ritual, transporting me into a higher state of awareness where my focus is heightened. I marvel at the physical manifestation (magic) before me and enter deeper into the moment, allowing my entire being to be taken by the flow of energy that I'm allowing in. The true bliss I feel from painting becomes so overwhelming that thinking seems more like a chore at this point, and so I continue to allow my hand to flit about as it pleases. Because of the intense state of presence I put myself in, without the outpouring of random thought forms, divine energy has a chance to work through me. The act of surrender allows me to do what I came here to do: send light and love into this world, experience the bliss, power and perfection that I already am. I expand with grace, ease and beauty as divine energy moves through my channels, clearing away blockages and toxic qi.

As you can see, creative practices can easily turn into profound spiritual rituals or healing sessions you can give yourself. After painting, I always look like I've just come out of a crystal healing session, complete with singing bowls, mantras, incense, Reiki attunements—the whole works!

Creating art literally opens your heart chakra and keeps you happy, youthful and strong. As you create, you actually draw in shen (soul) energy which works to heal the psyche, clear the upper chakras and enables you to express compassion.

The Different Forms of Qi

What is spiritual or formless energy? In Chinese medicine and Taoism you often hear of the three treasures which sustain human life: shen, qi, and jing.

Shen is associated with spiritual energy, the mind, the psyche and the upper dan tien, located at the third eye. Unlike the other types of qi, shen has to be cultivated with meditation and other spiritual practices. It can be nurtured with dancing and other creative activities that enable spiritual energy to flow through you. Performing art as a spiritual or magical ritual will increase shen energy. It's expressed as love, compassion, kindness and forgiveness. A high level of shen will be seen as a shimmer or brightness in the eyes.

Qi is an invisible force that enables the body to move and think. It's the most immediate source of energy for the body to use. It enters through the nose and circulates both energy and blood. It flows through the meridians in the body and if it becomes stagnant, physical illness can arise. Qigong, massage, proper diet and meditation can all improve qi flow. It is associated with the middle dan tien and the heart chakra.

Jing is associated with the kidneys, adrenals and the vitality and youthfulness of the physical body. It was passed to you from your parents at conception and is associated with the lower dan tien, just below the navel. Jing governs how your bones, teeth and hair grow. It is associated with mental processes and sexual maturity. After puberty, it controls fertility and clarity of mind. It circulates through the eight extraordinary channels and creates bone marrow and sexual fluids. Jing is depleted with too much stress, overuse of alcohol or drugs, illness, injury and poor nutrition. Loss of jing can be seen in mental degeneration, thinning or grey hair, or weak bones and teeth. When all the jing in a body is depleted, the body dies. Jing can be strengthened through proper nutrition, rest, meditation, qigong, herbal tonics and acupuncture. Now we know that we can also use our intention to restore energy levels!

The Kun Gong Energy Centre

I learned about the kun gong (pronounced kwun gawng) energy centre from Dr. and Master Zhi Gang Sha (www.drsha.com). It's a sacred energy centre located behind the navel that produces yuan jing (pronounced ywen jing), yuan qi (pronounced ywen chee) and yuan shen (pronounced ywen shun). Yuan means original, so yuan jing, yuan qi and yuan shen are original jing, original qi and original shen.

When a father's sperm and mother's egg unite, the Source (Tao) gives yuan shen (original soul energy) to the embryo. Yuan shen produces yuan jing and yuan qi. Yuan jing is the original matter. Yuan qi is the original energy. Together yuan shen, qi and jing are like the oil in a full oil lamp. As you age, however, this oil starts to deplete with stress and time.

Sun Meditation to Increase Yuan Qi, Yuan Jing and Yuan Shen

Go outside on a warm sunny day and sit somewhere you feel safe and comfortable where there is no one around. A forest would be suitable. If the weather doesn't permit, stay inside and imagine that you are in a forest on a warm summer day. Begin the meditation by closing your eyes and placing your hands on your navel, one on top of the other. Wherever you place your hands, energy will flow. Breathe in slowly through your nose and out through your mouth three times. Once you feel relaxed, take in a deep breath and imagine golden liquid light beaming from the sun into your crown. Watch the golden liquid light travel down your chakras to rest at your kun gong area. Imagine your kun gong is a honey pot and watch as the honey from the sun begins to ooze into the pot, coating the sides and resting at the bottom, one-third full. Breathe out and feel the warmth and power of the sun in your kun gong. Breathe in once more, drawing in more liquid light down through your head to flow through your body to finally rest in your kun gong area. Watch the honey pot fill with oozing liquid light, two-thirds full. Breathe out and feel the power of the sun radiating in your kun gong, the energy pulsing into your hands. Inhale and allow the liquid light to once again travel down to your kun gong, this time filling it to the brim. Breathe out and witness the power of the sun burning in your body. See your kun gong filled with brilliant shimmering light. Breathe in once more and draw in the liquid light down to your kun gong. This time, as you send the light down, the honey pot begins to overflow with honey. The power of the sun begins to fill your lower dan tien area, strengthening your foundation and connection to the Earth, empowering you to walk through the world fearlessly. Breathe out and witness the light of the sun beaming in your lower dan tien, travelling down into your legs and up into your chest. Breathe in the light of the sun and send it down into your kun gong one final time. This time, as the light hits the area, an explosion of light occurs and it sends the power of the sun throughout your whole body. Watch as the light travels up to your shoulders, down your arms and into your fingers. See it travel up your spine and into your head. Breathe out and watch the light shoot right out of your feet, spreading into your aura. Feel and witness your entire being strengthened and protected by the light of the sun. Repeat: "I am the power and strength of the sun. I am a sovereign being of light." Open your eyes and offer a prayer of thanks to the sun before returning to your day.

Dangers of Channelling

Because my creative practices have turned into spiritual rituals, I often call upon higher beings to work through me as I create. If you're going to channel while you create, it's always important to make sure you're grounded and your heart is open. You must psychically protect yourself and always set an intention before connecting. Although artists may claim that creating while intoxicated helps to give them inspiration, this is actually quite a dangerous practice if you're an energetically sensitive person. When you ingest drugs or alcohol of any kind, you may open spiritual channels or chakras, but not always in a safe way. In doing this, you can invite in lower level entities that operate in a service-to-self mode, who have absolutely no compassion for your own well-being. These entities only want to use you for your vital energy. Often these beings have been created by magicians, intentionally or unintentionally, through thought forms and emotions, and do not have the same type of energetic template that you have. They do not have the ability to manifest into a human form to experience the richness of a physical reality. They desire to feed off you to gain power as they do not have the same manifestation abilities that you have.

Psychic Protection for Spiritual Artists

Before you begin channelling through the act of creating art, it is imperative to protect yourself energetically. To do so, sit in meditation for as long as you need to until your entire body feels relaxed. Before you begin your meditation, you can ground yourself quickly by breathing in pink light through your crown chakra. While inhaling, send the light through your head into your heart chakra. On the exhale, send the light through your body, out your toes and down into the centre of the Earth. Inhale and send the light back up your legs to your heart. Exhale and send the light out to the universe to meet with the Source. Breathe in through your crown and your root chakra, shooting light from above and from below, once again to your heart chakra. Exhale and send the light out into your body, your aura, and all around you. You can use white light if you want to, but it's such a powerfully protective colour that it doesn't always let in the good spirits that want to work with you. Pink protects us from negative energy while safely inviting our angels and guides into our field.

After you're surrounded in light, do your best to let go of any story about who you are. Let your past go, along with any ideas for the future, including what your art should look like. Completely surrender to being, letting even your thoughts about the day go. Sit and observe your breath. If thoughts arise, say, "Thinking," and return to sensing your breath. This is a common Buddhist meditation practice that works like a charm to rid your mind of unwanted thought forms. Once you're completely still internally, it's time to set an intention.

You can now choose to invoke your higher self to work through you, or any other guides and angels you feel comfortable working with. For example, if you choose to invoke your higher self, with one hand on your heart and the other just beneath your navel, you could say: "I now command myself as God to channel my highest self into this form. Thank you."

If you're uncomfortable with the word God, you can use the term Source consciousness or call on any ascended master, guru, Buddha, etc., that you feel comfortable speaking to. The paramount thing when invoking is to feel a strong emotional connection to the power being called into your being. By placing your hand just beneath your navel, you remain grounded as you invoke, drawing power from your foundation to open your heart to receive spiritual energy and messages from the divine. By focusing on the heart, we access the soul and feel our connection to divinity.

It doesn't take years of quantum physics classes for us to discern that we are all of one consciousness. With the surrender into being it becomes obvious that we are all manifestations of the same Source. We can command ourselves from Source consciousness at any time by returning to the heart and using the mind to help us maintain focus and direct our energy.

As you begin your practice, don't worry about whether the spell you have cast upon yourself has worked or not. Indeed, it has and will be noticeable only if you surrender entirely to the moment and let go of all fear, all expectations and all attachments to outcomes. With this shedding of your humanity, your higher self now has the space to move through your form into this world.

As you create from the highest version of you, you may find yourself in an intense state of ecstasy. Often when you perform any activity at a master level, your brain will start to produce gamma brain waves.

Gamma waves are super subtle and incredibly fast. Originating in the thalamus (involved in controlling the motor systems of the brain), they move from the back of the brain to the front and back again 40 times per second. This sweeping motion puts you in a state of peak performance and high cognitive functioning where you are able to concentrate exceptionally well. If you've ever felt completely in touch with life, in a flow state where everything you do seems effortless, you've most likely been producing gamma waves.

Gamma waves increase memory recall while enhancing the senses. In the gamma state of consciousness, smells are stronger, food tastes better, colours are more vivid, hearing is sharpened and physical sensations are more enjoyable. In this state, you're able to receive information with extreme clarity, but also retain it and access it later with ease. People with high gamma activity are usually happier, calmer and more in tune with life. Low gamma waves have been associated with depression, learning difficulties and poor memory.

The good news is that meditation and doing activities that you love most will naturally boost gamma waves. Enter into your next creative practice as a magician and eternal student of life. Marvel at the movement of the vortex of light spinning through your physical vessel. Don't force the movement to adhere to the standards of your human ego. You are not a brain. You are not a body. You have a brain. You have a body. Surrender to the moment and feel yourself as consciousness spiralling through all dimensions and densities. Swim through time leisurely. You won't be in this physical form forever and there's nowhere else to go but here and now.

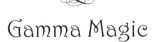

Gamma Magic

From the gamma state of consciousness, you can manifest quite easily. You've probably heard of the law of attraction or *The Secret,* about how we can create our world with our thoughts. This is partially true, as our thoughts do impact this world, but not all forces are under our control. There are certain phenomena such as the movement of the stars that we as humans have no control over. A true magician doesn't try to manipulate things out of his/her control, but rather asks what he/she can do with the things that he/she can control. With the breath, the body, the proper intention and emotion, mind is made manifest.

It is true that our thoughts do indeed become things. All things first start with a thought, a desire. This universe originally started with a desire from the divine to split itself into individuated parts in order to know itself.

When you manifest with thinking alone, this will achieve very little, as it's always the emotion behind the thought that actually sends the thought form into being. From the gamma state of consciousness, where you can access images with acute clarity and channel energy directly from Source, it's easy to see how manifestation would be much more effective. The clearer the intention, the stronger the magic. The stronger the magic, the stronger the manifestation into the physical.

White vs. Dark Magic

The act of using magic is the act of creation itself, of bringing spiritual energy into form. In every moment, whether you're conscious of it or not, you are using magic. Dark magic often comes about unintentionally from unconscious beings who are unaware that in every moment they're casting spells with their words, along with where they place their attention and intention. It is a noble thing indeed to perform white magic, which is simply manifestation that aligns with the will of your heart, your connection and way home to the divine. White magicians do not seek to control or manipulate their realities to serve themselves alone, but rather seek to express the will of God through their actions to benefit all souls.

Black magic is simply magic being done from a service-to-self standpoint which deviates from unconditional love. Often dark magicians are riddled with lower level entities that they've invited into their energy bodies unconsciously through the use of drugs and alcohol or through the storage of toxic emotion or thought forms, which attracts these beings. It is another thing entirely to do dark magic intentionally. This type of magic is done by sorcerers who aim to gain control over the forces we cannot control, such as the movement of the stars, the force of God itself. The darkest sorcery is that which aims to separate itself from God, from all souls, to obtain a false sense of power or control. It is clear to see that the majority of the leaders of our world are practicing intentional sorcery. Do not be fooled by the lure of feeding the ego alone. The service-to-self mode many humans still operate under unfortunately enforces the illusion or separation and ultimately cuts them off from unity consciousness. When people talk about Hollywood being Satanic in nature, this is precisely what they are referring to. This, of course, is an exercise in futility, for the ones stuck in the illusion will inevitably ascend back into the same Source we all do and realize they can never overpower another being, for there is no other.

The Power of Ritual

Rituals can be used as a drama we enact to trick the mind. The mind is an incredibly powerful problem solver, but also a tool that can be utilized to transcend ordinary consciousness. The dances performed by shamans for thousands upon thousands of years have always been used to help people escape the mundane, ordinary state of consciousness and enter into the spiritual world, to view life through the shamanic state of consciousness. The deeper we fall into the rituals we create, the more powerful our magic will be.

Magic rituals allow you to forget about the insatiable demands of the ego for a moment. They enable you to enter deeply into the present by stimulating all your physical senses, whereby the only choice left is to become one with the now, to enter into a thoughtless state of awe and wonder. Hollywood movies can also be seen as a form of magic, nowadays often crude versions of classical stories from ancient cultures.

When all your senses are stimulated and you lose the ability to think about what you're doing, instead merging into the oneness of the moment, it's here where your power lies. Thoughts still arise during ritual magic, but they flow so effortlessly they do not cause any distraction.

To transcend the mind, it's a wonderful idea to learn how to create an altar space to perform your magic rituals in.

Creating a Magic Altar Space

After a meditation where you've consciously taken time out of your busy schedule to sit in silence in order to recharge your form with divine energy, or after creating art as a spiritual practice, it's a wonderful time to use your magic. With the spiritual energy inside you flowing so effortlessly through your channels, your thought forms, emotions, attention and intention will be much easier to direct. Once again, before performing any magic ritual, it's always a good idea to protect yourself psychically and set an intention. Check-in with yourself by asking, "Why?" Why do you want to manifest what you do? Are your desires coming from your heart or your mind? The noblest magic is that which aligns with the will of your heart, which 100% of the time aligns with the will of God. Heart magic is effortless, divine and our innate right to utilize as creative beings.

Before casting any spell, it is imperative to create a sacred space for you to work in. In the same manner that meditators sit in the same quiet and comfortable place time-and-time again, often facing the same direction to meditate, so too does the magician enter into altered states of consciousness by entering into his/her sacred altar space. The mere sight of the traditional magical artifacts such as a candle or a wand immediately elicits a visceral response within the body of the magician that tells him/her that it's time to enter into the sacred. If ritual or ceremonial magic is practiced on a regular basis, your magic will be more powerful when a state of thoughtlessness is achieved, allowing the intuitive mind to reign.

Find a quiet place in your home where you can simply sit and relax without any interruption. Make sure you feel completely comfortable in this place. Get a small table and decorate it with objects, symbols and photos that make you happy and remind you of how fortunate you are to be alive. A candle is always a good idea to add to your altar, as it reminds you of the eternal flame that burns within you! A mirror will reflect that light back to the world. Fresh flowers and incense will also help elevate your mood and invite good energy. Personal photos of loved ones or spiritual teachers can help connect you to your heart. The possibilities are limitless with a sacred space. Add whatever objects make you smile and remind you of your divine nature.

To stimulate all your senses and enter into a state of extreme presence, whereby you're able to channel divine energy, you may choose to acquire certain magical objects.

Magical Essentials

- A wand to symbolize the mind and the element of air. A wand can be used to summon spiritual energy or to direct it. It is also often seen as a representation of the masculine and should be placed in the eastern section of your altar. You may also choose another object to represent air such as a feather, a wing or a fan.

- A chalice to symbolize the emotions and the element of water. A chalice can be used to hold ceremonially blessed or charged liquid, and is often looked at as a representation of the feminine, in particular the womb. A chalice should be placed in the western section of your altar. You may also choose another object to represent water such as a shell, a starfish or a piece of coral.

- An athame (dagger) to symbolize the spirit and the element of fire. An athame, a masculine symbol, can be used to cut energetic cords, to carve sigils into candles, or to safely enter and exit sacred circles. An athame should be placed in the southern section of your altar. You may also choose another object to represent fire such as a candle, a match or a symbol of the sun.

- A pentacle to symbolize the physical and the element of earth. A pentacle representing both the feminine and masculine and beyond, is used to bring the magician into harmony with all four elements and spirit itself. A pentacle should be placed in the northern section of your altar. You may also choose another object to represent earth such as a stone, a piece of bark or a leaf.

Other Magical Objects to Add to Your Ritual Space

- A vial of holy oil, usually made from olives, to consecrate the altar space and magic objects to match your intent.
- A bell to invoke or banish spiritual forces.
- A magical journal to record spells and their efficacy.
- An oil lamp or candle placed in the centre of the altar to draw in energy from the elemental portals and to create a gateway between worlds. Another pentacle can be placed beneath the centre oil lamp/candle with a lamp directly overhead, representing the as above/so below cosmic principle.

- A black cloth to lay over the altar table to represent the spiritual realm, the unmanifest.

- Coloured candles for spell casting.

- Candles to represent the divine feminine and divine masculine. These candles should be placed away from the centre oil lamp/candle to create a triangle. The goddess candle is red, while the god candle is black. They represent the first emanations from Source.

- Images of your favourite deities can be placed next to the god and goddess candles along with anything else that feels right to you. It is much more important for your altar space to personally elicit a powerful emotional response within you than it is to align with someone else's idea of magical perfection.

- A representation of a human skull placed in between the deity images to symbolize the knowledge of our ancestors who passed down occult knowledge of the mystery traditions. A black candle is placed on the skull from the autumn to spring equinox. A red candle is used from the spring to autumn equinox. Black represents the knowledge contained within the spiritual realm while red symbolizes that knowledge flowing to us. Depending on the time of year, the candle placed upon the skull will either match the god or goddess candle.

- A cauldron, placed in front of the skull, to symbolize the womb of the goddess and to perform scrying and fire magic in.

Magical Clothing Items Can Include:

- A crown to affirm your divinity.
- A robe to symbolize simplicity and silence.
- A lamen (magical pendant) worn at the level of the heart for protection and also to signify your divine authority. Specific crystals can be used to evoke specific spiritual energy or to commune with certain deities.

In Ceremonial Magic, These Items are Also Used in Some Traditions:

- A scourge (a whip used for self-mortification), a dagger and a chain. These objects are placed around the magician to keep his/her intent pure.

Once you have your altar space items, you can then create your altar and easily evoke the elements to help you manifest. To do this, you will need to acquire objects associated with each element: a rock, incense, a candle and match, and a small bowl of water. These objects should be placed near you, so you don't have to get up to retrieve them as you're invoking.

Working with the Elements

In order to be in your full power, you must learn to work with elemental energies. Understanding what each element represents and how to work with it is essential to your magical practice. The elements earth, air, fire, water and spirit are the foundation of the reality you see. Learning when to call upon specific elements in your spell casting can increase your ability to manifest your desired reality.

Calling upon earth would help ground you and centre you in your physical body, reminding you that true wealth comes from within. Having a strong connection to the element earth is essential for money spells and planning. Invoking air would help you increase your mental clarity, which would help you focus for a test. Fire can revitalize romantic relationships or inspire you to take action to manifest your dreams. Along with purification, water can help bring fluidity to any situation. Use your intuition when working with the elements. You can also use them to banish or purify unwanted energy. Earth can be used to bury, air can be used to blow away, fire can be used to burn and water can be used to drown.

If you receive an idea from spirit, you use your mind (air) to set an intention. You feel excited about the idea (water) and make a plan (earth). Then you take action (fire). Without proper knowledge of how to use the elements, you can remain trapped in thinking and never actually materialize your ideas. A true magician is always an elemental alchemist.

Earth represents the physical realm and senses, nature, good health, fertility, strength, abundance, gnomes, elves and four-legged creatures.

Air represents the mental realm and intellect, wisdom, communication, ability to listen, knowledge, clear thinking and perspective, prayer, meditation, fairies, angels and winged creatures.

Fire represents the action realm, movement, transformation, passion, sexuality, illumination, ecstasy, the use of power, joy, purpose, warmth, energy, willpower, phoenix, dragons, lions, salamanders and other fiery creatures.

Water represents the emotional realm, intuition, psychic abilities, clear emotions, friendship, harmonious relationships, receiving and giving love or guidance, fluidity, adaptability, rejuvenation, regeneration, dolphins, whales, mermaids, sprites and other water creatures.

Experiment with each element. If you're usually a mental person, venture into the forest and sit with the trees to ground yourself. Ask the earth a question and pick up a rock to inspect it for subtle hints. Bathe in a river and ask the spirits who live there to help you empathize or become more flexible. Dance around a fire and watch how the flames burn without restraint. Ask them to energize you or transform your apathy into passion. Raise your arms and feel the wind at your back, gently pushing you in the direction of truth. Ask the breeze to clear your mind of unwanted thoughts or attachments. Allow it to impregnate you with visionary insights and clear thinking.

There is not just one way to work with the elements. Follow your passion and always trust in your intuition. Realize deeply that because nature is creative, you, who contains all the same elements nature does, are also a creative genius. Aligning with the elements enables you to align with the power of God, to become a conscious co-creator of your reality. Let the manifesting begin!

Invoking the Elements

Before beginning any magical practice, invoke each element to balance your energies and empower yourself to manifest from a place of purity and strength. You are free to adjust the following invocations as you please and add any other magical objects that you feel comfortable working with. Your magical objects should elicit a powerful response in you when you gaze upon them. They should make you feel comfortable, safe, joyful and confident. If they don't, find new objects!

To begin, place your wand on the eastern portion of the altar while thinking of the element air. You can say something such as: *"Here is the wand to represent the element of air."* Then place the incense on the altar and light it. Wait for the smoke to clear, lightly blowing into it to allow it to be dispersed over the altar space. As you watch the smoke, repeat something such as: *"Air is movement, flow and freedom."* Look at the wand and say: *"Here is the wand to represent the element of air. Air is movement, flow and freedom."*

Place your athame (dagger) on the southern portion of the altar while thinking of the element fire. You can say something such as: *"Here is the athame to represent the element of fire."* Then place the candle on the altar and light it with a match. Pass your left hand over the flame so you can feel its heat. As you feel the heat, repeat: *"Fire is passion, inspiration and transformation."* Look at the dagger and say: *"Here is the athame to represent the element of fire. Fire is passion, inspiration and transformation."*

Place the chalice on the western portion of the altar while thinking of the element water. You can say something such as: *"Here is the chalice to represent the element of water."* Then place the bowl of water on the altar and dip your left hand (palm up) into the water.

Cup your hand and slowly lift it out of the water, allowing the water to move through your fingers back into the bowl. As the water trickles, repeat: *"Water is purification, adaptation and magnetism."* Look at the chalice and say: *"Here is the chalice to represent the element of water. Water is purification, adaptation and magnetism."*

Place the pentacle on the northern portion of the altar while thinking of the element earth. You can say something such as: *"Here is the pentacle to represent the element of earth."* Then pick up the rock and squeeze it in your hand. Hold the rock between both your palms, feeling its texture and temperature. As you feel the aliveness within the rock, repeat: *"Earth is form, foundation and strength."* Look at the pentacle and say: *"Here is the pentacle to represent the element of earth. Earth is form, foundation and strength."*

Once all items are placed on your altar, any words you speak will be imbued with the elemental forces you've evoked.

According to Native American shamanism, the east is associated to air, spring, innocence and birth. The south is associated to fire, summer and manifestation. The west is associated to water, fall and transformation. The north is associated to earth, winter and death. There are many different shamanic or magical practices that invoke the elements or directions in a slightly different way. Trust in your intuition and don't be afraid to experiment.

Ceremonial Elemental Invocations

If you aren't at an altar and want to invoke the elements in a group, you can do so with verbal invocations. As you speak, you may choose to have everyone face each direction associated to the elements.

To invoke the element of air and the direction east, repeat: "We invite the direction of east and the element of air, the mental realm, to our circle. We thank you, air, for breathing life into us, for providing us with wisdom, clarity of mind and the ability to consciously create our lives. We thank you for blessing us with clear thoughts, communication and beliefs. We call upon the butterflies, the birds, the fairies, the angels and the winged ones to bless us with the clarity to express our powerful insights. We invoke the element of air to bring us clarity of mind. We thank you for your guidance. We command ourselves as an aspect of God to claim the power of air, so we may speak the truth and align our intentions with the highest good of all."

To invoke the element of fire and the direction south, repeat: "We invite the direction of south and the element of fire, the action realm, to our circle. We thank you, fire, for inspiring us to take action, for providing us with passion, excitement, sexuality, vitality and growth. We thank you for blessing us with the ability to manifest lives in alignment with our soul. We call upon the dragons, the phoenix, the salamanders, the brave ones to bless us with the courage to express our authentic selves. We invoke the power of the sun to illuminate the truth and bring clarity of spirit. We thank you for your guidance. We command ourselves as an aspect of God to claim the power of fire so we may manifest our desires and align our intentions with the highest good of all."

To invoke the element of water and the direction west, repeat: "We invite the direction of west and the element of water, the emotional realm, to our circle. We thank you, water, for enabling us to empathize, for providing us with emotional maturity, wisdom and adaptability. We thank you for blessing us with the ability to discern, to respond rather than react. We call upon the sprites, mermaids, dolphins, whales and other sea creatures to bless us with the power to give and receive love. We invoke the element of water to bring clarity of heart. We thank you for your guidance. We command ourselves as an aspect of God to claim the power of water so we may navigate with clarity, reflecting the highest love, and align our intentions with the highest good of all."

To invoke the element of earth and the direction north, repeat: "We invite the direction of north and the element of earth, the physical realm, to our circle. We thank you, earth, for enabling us to enjoy our physical senses, for providing us with strength, health and a connection to nature. We thank you for blessing us with the ability to feel safe in our bodies, deeply in tune with the internal and external rhythms of nature. We call upon the bears, the horses, the gnomes and all the four-legged creatures of Earth. We invoke the element of earth to strengthen our foundation and vital energy. We thank you for your guidance. We command ourselves as an aspect of God to claim the power of earth so we may live in harmony with the natural world and align our intentions with the highest good of all."

Elemental Intentions

If you're an energetically sensitive person, an empath, it's a good idea to invoke the elements each morning to help keep you centred in your own body. To do so, repeat the following:

"Air, I love you with all my soul. As an aspect of God, I command you to only think my thoughts of the highest order. Fire, I love you with all my soul. As an aspect of God, I command you to only feel my passion, sexuality and inspiration of the highest order. Water, I love you with all my soul. As an aspect of God,

I command you to only feel my emotions and intuition of the highest order. Earth, I love you with all my soul. As an aspect of God, I command you to only feel my senses of the highest order and stand my ground in alignment with Source. Spirit, I love you with all my soul. As an aspect of God, I command you to only make choices in alignment with my highest good, with Source, and so it is."

Moon Magic

Knowing which phase the moon is in can be tremendously important for spell casting. On new moons, it's wise to cast spells that have to do with beginnings. For example, if you want to draw in a lot of abundance and create a life filled with wealth, casting a spell on the new moon is a good idea. Full moons are associated to endings or completions, and are the perfect time to cast spells that have to do with letting go. If you want to let go of bad habits, emotions or even negative people, full moons are a wonderful time to purge toxic energy from your experience. Studying the heavenly bodies can be very helpful in spell-work as they act like portals for higher dimensional information to flow. If you were to cast a spell with a moon in Taurus, which represents money, business, beauty and love, it would be much more effective than casting the same spell with the moon in another less practical sign such as Pisces. Use your intuition and have fun with your casting. If you're enjoying yourself completely, your magic will be much stronger.

Knowing which planets are retrograde can be very helpful when casting spells as well. If you cast a money spell when Jupiter or Venus is retrograde, it won't be as effective. Retrogrades turn energy inward and often put external success on hold. Learning which elements, archetypes and ideas each planet represents can help you align your desires with the desires of the universe. It's much easier to flow with the current of heavenly magic than to fight against it creating something out of alignment with Source.

Astro Magic

Study the zodiac signs and their meanings to aid you in your magic practice.

Aries

Cardinal fire, ruled by Mars

Impulsiveness, leadership, intuition, willpower, war, courage, inspiration, acting without thinking, playfulness

Taurus

Fixed earth, ruled by Venus

Beauty, money, business, sex without emotional connection, pleasure, physical senses, nature, stubbornness, security, comfort

Gemini

Mutable air, ruled by Mercury

The mind, communication, creativity, lack of consistency, technology, singing, learning, direct environment, playfulness, lack of focus

Cancer

Cardinal water, ruled by the Moon

Emotions, comfort, music, stubbornness, over-sensitivity, beauty, creating a beautiful home, nurturing, the mother, strong intuition

Leo

Fixed fire, ruled by the Sun

Drama, passion, the heart, generosity, leadership, the limelight, self-centredness, glamour, creative expression

Virgo

Mutable earth, ruled by Mercury

The mind, precision, details, worry, daily tasks, utility, criticism, purity, sacredness, cleanliness, over-thinking

Libra

Cardinal air, ruled by Venus

Beauty, balance, relationships, weak sense of individuated self, peace, justice, vanity, harmony, creative self-expression

Scorpio

Fixed water, ruled by Pluto

Emotional intensity, power, control, mind-games, extreme situations, truth, transformation, darkness, music, strong intuition

Sagittarius

Mutable fire, ruled by Jupiter

Freedom, learning, teaching, authority, fixed thinking, travel, joy, exploring other lands and cultures, strong sex drive, rule-making

Capricorn

Cardinal earth, ruled by Saturn

Stability, structure, order, authority, introversion, emotional maturity, ambitious, power, strength, persistence, rigidness, lack of playfulness

Aquarius

Fixed air, ruled by Uranus

Communication, the mind, fixed thinking, humanitarianism, visionary insights, non-attachment, music, creative self-expression, out-of-the-box thinking, teaching

Pisces

Mutable water, ruled by Neptune

Emotions, sensitivity, spirit, other realms, imagination, magic, lying, detachment, creative self-expression, music, strong intuitive abilities

Study the planets and their meanings to aid you in your magic practice.

Sun

The Sun represents your ego or personality. It shows how likely you are to assert yourself and describes the lens from which you view the world. It can also be the fuel that powers you. Associated sign: Leo.

Moon

The Moon represents how you will interact with others emotionally. Your imagination, intuition, receptivity, adaptability and ability to empathize will be influenced by the Moon. The

Moon also shows you where you've come from in previous lifetimes. Associated sign: Cancer.

Mercury

Mercury represents your intellect, common sense, learning and ability to communicate. Associated signs: Gemini and Virgo.

Venus

Venus gives you a sense of beauty, sociability and creativity. It shows you how you're likely to act in relationships of all kinds. Associate signs: Taurus and Libra.

Mars

Mars represents your vital energy, willpower and sexual drive. It shows you how courageous, impulsive or aggressive you can be. Associates sign: Aries.

Jupiter

Jupiter represents hope, optimism, learning, teaching, justice, philosophy and spiritual expansion. Associated sign: Sagittarius.

Saturn

Saturn illustrates what your harsh life lessons will be. It represents the physical world and all the demands, challenges and fears associated. Power, authority, endurance, concentration and caution are major themes. Associated sign: Capricorn.

Uranus

Uranus represents inspiration, creativity, sudden bursts of genius, spiritual awakenings and the strange or taboo. Sign associated: Aquarius.

Neptune

Neptune represents the spirit world, the unmanifest, intuition, dreams, magic, fantasy, illusion and dreams. Drugs or altered states of consciousness can also be major themes. Associated sign: Pisces.

Pluto

Pluto shows you how you deal with power. It represents your soul theme and where you will embrace and share your power, transforming yourself and the world. It deals with themes of transformation, death, re-birth, endurance, darkness, depth and spiritual truth. Associated sign: Scorpio.

For a more in-depth look into astrology, head to www.astro.com

Neuro-Linguistic Programming (NLP) Magic

NLP was created by Richard Bandler and John Grinder in the 1970s as an alternative therapy to help people re-program their brains and achieve goals. NLP uses the connection between neurological processes (neuro) and language (linguistic) to remove harmful engrained patterns of behaviour or transform them into positive ones.

The brain never shuts off. While you idly gaze out a window, your brain records the music playing in the background, the conversations occurring around you, along with how your body is responding to the stimuli. Media experts know this to be true and don't think twice about spending millions of dollars on Super Bowl commercials! Even if you're not paying conscious attention, your subconscious mind is.

Have you ever heard a song on the radio that reminded you of a particular nasty ex? Perhaps you were instantly flooded with memories of a face you'd rather forget while your body responded with anger or disgust. This is the subconscious mind resurfacing to protect you from future pain. While the song may have nothing to do with your ex, just the mere mention of it can drive you up a wall and trigger you into an hour-long lecture about how awful the person was to you.

Since the brain never shuts off, connections or neuro-associations are constantly being made. If you listen to a song that elicits a strong emotional response in your body and you think, *I love this song so much. It makes me so happy,* whenever you hear that song, your brain will fire in a specific way, shooting happy chemicals along a familiar neuro-pathway.

The Real Secret

Thoughts create things is a very common adage in the New Age community. On a scientific level, there is truth to this statement. When you think happy thoughts your brain literally creates the reward drug, dopamine. Your gastrointestinal system also plays a major role in your state of being, the bacteria inside responding to the same neurochemicals that the brain does: serotonin, GABA, norepinephrine, dopamine, acetylcholine and melatonin. When you think happy thoughts, your gut listens and in turn sends information to the brain to create a happy mood.

Nerve nets that repeatedly fire together, wire together. The good news is that your brain doesn't know the difference between mental and physical rehearsal. If you want to change a habit, simply imagining yourself acting in a new way will start changing the way your brain fires. Through simple observation it's clear to see that the stronger your imagination is, the more powerful your manifestations will be. Another reason to strengthen your ability to concentrate through meditation and enhance your clarity of vision with conscious daydreaming.

It takes some people longer than others to change their habits of behaviour, but the ones who seem to learn more quickly than others are most definitely tapping into their unconscious minds to create new neuro-associations.

To change a pattern of thought that is triggering you into a whirlwind of emotional pain, you want to address your most common negative thought. Spend some time analyzing what negative limiting belief you say to yourself most often. A common one for everyone is, *I'm not good enough*, so we'll work on that. Say it out loud right now. See how silly it sounds repeated in this way? In doing this, you instantly tell your brain that you can consciously choose to place awareness on the thought or not. Consciously choosing to place attention on your bad thoughts will not bring bad things into your life. The real secret to life is to face your fears and see that anything painful arising is there to help you heal and return you to a heart-centred path.

You can choose to dig into your limiting beliefs by questioning: *Is it true? Who told it to me? Why am I holding onto it if it isn't bringing me joy? Who would I be and what would my life look like without the thought?* Once you know the origin of the thought it will be much easier to extricate it from your mind. It will no longer arise at inappropriate times to seek your loving attention.

The emotion associated with the limiting belief may still linger, however, and if you get triggered into feeling not good enough, the thought may arise unconsciously as a response to the pain. This can create an endless cycle of addiction to pain, to the chemicals the brain produces when you're in pain. Even if the pain is uncomfortable, the instability or fear of the unknown may be even more terrifying. Attaching to painful thoughts or emotions is a safety mechanism that keeps you perpetually trapped in cycles of unconscious, destructive behaviour.

Responses to painful situations are usually learned and repeated patterns of behaviour. It becomes an unconscious choice to allow your external circumstances to dictate how you feel. With intentional journeying into the subconscious, you can free yourself from enslavement to your own reactions. You can create space to choose not to react to negative forces or give any attention to that which doesn't serve you.

To break free, consciously choose to face your pain. Think the thought, *I'm not good enough*, and focus on the feeling it creates inside your body. Do you feel contracted, tense or filled with internal heat? Good! Continue to narrow in on the sensation the thought creates within you. If you're really overwhelmed and need to calm down a bit, perform the **5D Healing Technique: It's Safe to Feel**. Tell the emotion, "It's okay that you're here. You have a right to be here. You are worthy of being here. I love you."

Your state of emotional well-being is determined by two things: your thoughts and how you hold your body. Think about it logically. If you sit slumped over thinking, *I suck at everything*, you aren't going to feel your best. If you get up and jump up-and-down and think, *I'm so awesome and totally rock*, you'll be filled with excitement. It's easy to see how you can change your emotions through the conscious use of language, movement and imagination.

Though it may feel strange at first to consciously choose a positive thought when you're feeling low, it may be easier to do this if you're jumping up-and-down or dancing to your favourite song. If you're stuck on a low emotional vibration, it's not thinking alone that will change your state. It's going to be the shift in energy that will return you to your peace. To shift your energy, you have to get moving. Here's where it gets interesting.

If you look at the brain like a super computer that can be programmed by your consciousness, with awareness you can discern what patterns of behaviour are like viruses that need to be deleted from your memory. If your brain is the hardware, why not update it with the latest and greatest software?

When the thought, *I'm not good enough*, arises, instead of playing out the same old patterns of behavior: hunching over depressed or falling into your own self-imposed pit of despair, consciously focus on the thought. Invite it to be with you. Send it whatever it needs to transform into peace. Now, use your body to get up and move. Dance, shake, wiggle and hop until the thought is completely flushed from your system. As you're moving, think a positive thought. The combination of movement and positive thinking will instantly help shift you into a higher emotional state and save you from being triggered any further.

Realize deeply that worrying will never bring you closer to your goals or solve your problems. Remain the witness and when you catch yourself stuck in a thought pattern, breathe deeply and return to the present. Consciously choose to let go.

If you find it difficult to break free from intense emotional pain, ask yourself, "Am I being totally honest about how I feel?"

Simply stating out loud, "I'm scared. I don't know what's going to happen. I don't feel well. I don't know which direction to take," can provide you with the instant relief you're looking for. When you're completely honest about how you feel in any given moment, your emotions or thoughts are allowed to exist as they are. Often the loving attention you give to your own darkness helps to transmute it back into the peace it comes from. This radical honesty isn't weak and it will never bring you more of what you do not desire. On the contrary, it will provide you with all the answers you're looking for, and usually a solution to a difficult situation. Love heals all blockages within the body, mind, spirit and heart.

Train Your Brain

To eliminate persistent triggers or viruses you may want to include what coach extraordinaire Tony Robbins calls an anchor: an activity that you do that instantly triggers you to feel a specific emotion; something that elicits strong positive thoughts and pleasurable sensations in your body. An anchor can be something as simple as snapping or clapping. I personally snap to let my brain know something is extra important and to pay extra attention. I've snapped so many times while memorizing speeches that my brain instantly pays more attention when I snap now. If that isn't real magic, I don't know what is!

I've noticed that whenever I'm really excited about something, a new job, a new friend, a new business opportunity, etc., I tend to pull my arms into my chest and shake them really quickly back and forth while smiling, squealing and laughing. I use this exact anchor now to enable myself to feel excited whenever I need to.

To pull yourself out of a low emotional state, you can always add in humour to re-program yourself. What would happen if every time you got into a fight with someone, you had the awareness to slow down and consciously choose to do something funny? The next time you're triggered into battling with a family member, consciously choose to slow your breath and return to your body. Feel the aliveness within your body by dancing. The stranger the moves, the better. The idea is to break the endless cycle of pain with something hilarious that causes everyone involved to start laughing. Laughing instantly raises your vibration and helps open the heart. By opening the heart and returning to the soul, negative emotions or thoughts naturally dissipate. Sometimes, all you have to do to return to feeling happy again is forget to think!

While this mode of operation may be slightly embarrassing at first, especially if you perform your anchors in public, I encourage you to explore it. As creatures of habit, it's up to us to choose habits that enable us to live healthy and abundant lives. The next time someone decides to project their pain onto you, stay present. Slow your breath and stay deeply connected to the aliveness within your body. Remember, when you're being attacked it's never personal. It's only a reflection of how disconnected the attacker is from his/her own heart. Send love to the person in pain by complimenting them. "Thank you for caring so much about how I affect you. It means a lot to me that you feel comfortable enough to share how you're feeling with me. I feel honoured to receive your attention." This response usually catches the attacker off guard and immediately helps him/her return to the heart.

Choose Joy!

We are powerful beings with limitless potential for creation. When we choose to take responsibility for our lives and consciously choose to create them, every moment becomes a gift, an opportunity to send more love into this world.

Though at first it may feel or appear strange to others or to yourself to choose happiness, it is a necessary choice to make if you want to live well. As individuals, we've chosen to give our power away to institutions that have absolutely no concern for our well-being and instead view us as profitable resources—cogs in the corporate machine.

We've been fed lies from the media about how we're not complete and need to buy our happiness, when in reality if we do even the smallest amount of spiritual exploration, we are able to clearly observe that we're already whole.

Sometimes negative thoughts or harmful patterns of behaviour stem from placing too much emphasis on the material world. When you view yourself solely as a physical being, it becomes very easy to fall into the trap of not being good enough or not having enough. This is why it's absolutely necessary to return to the truth of your being, which isn't a thing at all. The nothingness, the stillness and silence that you come from, that you will return to, is always with you. The peace you seek externally can always be found with a cessation of thinking and a return to the breath. It arises effortlessly and greets you humbly without any expectation.

The way out of pain is to go within.

Meditation

Meditation is a release into the field of awareness itself. When you consciously choose to shut off the mind and simply sense the ever-present flow of breath, you see that you are being breathed into this existence. "Who is being breathed?" you may ask. The mind will usually yell out, "Me, me! I'm the one in charge." Take no notice of the passing thoughts, of the automatic function of thinking. Meditation is a release into the unknown, the unseen worlds from which you come. It is a merging back into the peace, love and bliss that you already are.

What is leftover when you no longer attach to your thoughts and instead treat them as passing bubbles within the endless stream of consciousness? Who is leftover? Who is looking through your eyes? Who is feeling with your heart? Who is hearing with your ears? Who is sensing with your fingers? Who is smelling with your nose? Who is tasting with your tongue? Who is witnessing the emergence of light into this world? Who is the presence that dwells within you and within all beings and all things?

When you give yourself a break from thinking, it's clear that there is still intelligence within you, an observer that uses the mind and heart as tools. An eternal consciousness that cannot be killed, cannot be hurt and does not know fear or lack. Without an addiction to thinking your inner awareness has a chance to arise. The observer of life has room to play. By simply sitting in silence and darkness, without thought, observe that you are still able to *exist* without the mind. What does this mean? You are *not* your mind. Yet there is still an intelligence with you that will never leave. A force that already knows everything you're seeking externally.

With a return to silence, your true essence can be experienced. Without the attachment to thinking, which causes suffering, you are left with true joy, peace, bliss, completion and love. You see that since you *are* love itself, nothing outside of you will ever bring you more love. You are the love that you're seeking and in order to return to that love, you must give it away freely through unconditional service to others who are a part of the oneness that you are.

When you dedicate your life to service and to the creator, through offering your heart to those around you without expecting anything in return, fear and suffering cease. Anything you're seeking you see indeed comes from within. The material objects you desire to feel certain emotions are no longer necessary as you realize you can create any emotion you desire in the moment, by giving it away freely. The kingdom of heaven has always been within.

Through meditation you access the eternal and often lose touch with what is you and what is the other. It is common during your practice to lose your sense of individuated identity, which may bring some fear. This fear, however, is only the fear of death—the death of your ego, your individuated self.

Meditation is a wonderful time to question your identity. Who would you be without your gender? Would you still exist without your role as a mother, a teacher, a lover? Would you still be as worthy of love, as important, if you suddenly lost all your possessions, your income? Who would you be without your clothes, your image, even your personality? Would you still exist without any of these things? Would you in fact still exist without a body? What are you? Who are you? Where did you come from? Why are you here?

This self-inquiry will always lead you to your true self, which is nothingness. It becomes very apparent through the practice of meditation that you are not your thoughts, not your passing emotions, not even your physical form.

So what are you? If you lose your left foot in a car accident, are you now less of a person? No, because you are not your body. You are consciousness using the body. Using the brain. Using the heart. Often we associate thinking with intelligence, but consciousness is not concentrated in the mind alone. It is clear that the heart and gastrointestinal system are also brains.

Heart and Brain Coherence

The bacteria in your gut both produce and respond to the same neurochemicals found in the brain. When you think a thought, your gut and immune system is listening and responding accordingly. Your gut feelings are also getting sent to the brain. Meanwhile, the heart is also taking in information and responding to orders sent from the brain. Current research shows, however, that the heart actually sends more information to the brain than the brain sends to the heart! With the 40, 000 neurons the heart contains, it's clear that the organ we previously thought of as something only pumping blood, is actually an intelligent system that can learn and hold memories. The heart is also a hormonal gland, producing neurotransmitters found in the brain such as oxytocin, the bonding hormone.

The HeartMath Institute (www.heartmath.org) research shows us that the patterns of heart activity can directly affect cognitive and emotional functioning. If you're stressed, for example, and your heart rhythm is erratic or too fast paced, the corresponding neural signals that travel to the brain from the heart actually prevent you from higher cognitive functioning. Stress stops you from thinking clearly and can limit your ability to remember, reason, learn or make decisions aligned with your highest good. This explains why we make rash decisions that harm us when we are under stress.

The wonderful news is that the opposite is also true; when your heart is beating regularly, it helps to facilitate positive emotions and allows for clear cognitive functioning. Maintaining heart and brain coherence can be achieved through simple breathing exercises. By taking in three deep, slow breaths at least five seconds in length and exhaling in the same fashion, the heart usually returns to a regular, peaceful rhythm.

The heart generates an electromagnetic field that is about 60 times greater in amplitude than the waves your brain emits. The EM field emitted is so powerful that it can be detected and measured several feet away from a person's body. The first thing anyone notices about you is your heart, whether they're aware of it or not. The field you emit instantly tells someone whether you're in a loving or fearful state. This brings a whole new meaning to being magnetically attracted to someone.

Mantras

Since the brain, heart and enteric systems are all, in fact, brains (in that they produce hormones that help facilitate our mood), it's a good idea to test mantras on all three. Mantras are sacred sounds or sentences that have spiritual powers. Often, they're ancient sounds, thousands of years old, that have been repeated over and over again, imbued with the intention and power of spiritual seekers and masters. Sometimes they're used to tune specific areas of the energetic body. If you look at the body like an instrument, since in essence we're energy, it's easy to comprehend how we could use sound to heal. There's no doubt in my mind that the future of medicine will involve sound healing. That is, if the medical industries start focusing on healing rather than profit.

Mantras can also be used as a vehicle to enter deeper into consciousness. When you sit in meditation and focus all your attention on the sound you're creating, you give your mind something to watch. Over time, as you continue to chant the sacred sound internally or externally, you merge deeper and deeper into the sound until you become the sound itself. You temporarily lose track of your personality, your physical body and your never-ending-to-do-list. The mantra allows you to transcend the mind, to transcend your humanity, to enter into the field of awareness that you come from, that you are. When you connect to this place, a healing naturally occurs. You merge with the infinite fount of love and power that seeks to manifest itself through you. On a scientific level, miraculous things are also occurring.

Scientific Benefits of Meditation

Let's look at some important parts of the brain, and how meditation can change and benefit them:

1. Lateral prefrontal cortex

This is the part of the brain that deals with logic and reasoning. It allows us to make rational decisions and choices without falling back on automatic behaviours based on emotional responses. It is also called the assessment centre.

2. The medial prefrontal cortex

This is the "me centre" of the brain. It is the part that references our experiences and perspectives when dealing with new situations, in new social settings, or when just thinking about ourselves and our lives. It is this part that enables us to experience empathy and consider another person's state of mind.

The medial prefrontal cortex consists of two parts: the ventromedial medial prefrontal cortex (vmPFC), which is "involved in processing information related to you and people that you view as *similar* to you. This is the part of the brain that can cause you to end up taking things too personally."[10]

The second part is called the dorsomedial prefrontal cortex (dmPFC), which is "involved in processing information related to people who you perceive as being *dissimilar* from you. This very important part of the brain is involved in feeling empathy (especially for people who we perceive of as not being like us) and maintaining social connections."[11]

The insula and the amygdala also have important roles to play. While the insula monitors bodily sensations, and helps determine how strongly we will react to those sensations, the amygdala, our fear centre, is responsible for our fight-or-flight response.

With a regular meditation practice the unhealthy neural connections between the me centre and bodily sensations/fear centers of the brain

---

[10] Rebecca Gladding, "This Is Your Brain on Meditation," last modified March 22, 2013, https://www.psychologytoday.com/blog/use-your-mind-change-your-brain/201305/is-your-brain-meditation.

[11] Gladding (2013), *op. cit.* (note 10)

can weaken. Meanwhile, a healthy connection forms between the assessment center and bodily sensations/fear centers. You start to realize that when uncomfortable momentary bodily sensations of fear arise, they actually have nothing to do with you. This enables you to rationally determine that your own, or another person's pain, is not your personal problem. You see pain for what it is: a sensation, an indicator and nothing more. Because the good connections between these centres grow stronger, you're able to experience more empathy. Since other people are no longer hurting you and nothing is personal, you're able to remain calm and connected to the oneness that you are. Social anxiety and depression fades and in place of it, a true appreciation and excitement for being alive arises.

Sanskrit Mantras

Below is a list of my favourite Sanskrit mantras. Use the mantras you feel most drawn to and remember to speak them to each brain in your body. The appropriate mantra for you will be one that feels comfortable in your gut, heart and brain. Once you've found the mantra that brings you the most joy in all three areas, I encourage you to sit with it for at least 10 minutes a day. Working your way up to 20 minutes is even more beneficial. Sitting with mantras can be as simple as you want it to be. On the in-breath, you can repeat half the mantra and on the out-breath you can finish off the rest. Or you may choose to take in a breath and repeat the entire mantra on the out-breath. Whatever way feels best to you, is the best way for you to practice.

So hum: *I am that.*

Aham Prema (ah-hum pray-mah): I am love of the highest order. I am divine love.

Moksha (moke-sha): Freedom from suffering. Release from the cycle of death and rebirth.

Om Namah Shivaya (om nama shivaya): I bow to my true self, the God within me. I bow to Shiva, the supreme deity of transformation who represents the highest self.

Aham Brahmasmi (aham brahmas-mi): The core of my being is the ultimate reality, the root and ground of the Source of all that exists.

Om Gum Shrim Maha Lakshmiyei Swaha (om gum shreem maha lakshmi-yay swaha): Ganesha remove obstacles so Lakshmi can bring abundance.

Satcitananda (sat chit ananda): Truth/existence, consciousness, bliss. The true reality.

Om Radha Krishnaya Namaha (om rad-ha krish-nigh-ya na-ma-ha): For beautiful spiritual relationships.

Om Shree Dhanvantre Namaha (om shree dhan-van-tray na-ma-ha): Healing on all levels for self and others.

Om Namo Narayanaya (om namo nar-ayay-nigh-ya): The mantra of Vishnu chanted to invoke His all-pervading power of mercy and goodness. This mantra brings love, prosperity, wisdom and freedom from attachment to ego. It is a mantra of peace for all.

Are You Actually Physical?

A daily meditation practice allows you to witness what kind of thoughts or emotions you're holding inside you, sometimes unconsciously. You may be surprised to discover that traumas from childhood are still affecting your choices and actions today. Or perhaps you're making decisions that someone on the television told you to make. With silence comes the awareness to witness where your intentions are coming from. If limiting beliefs or negative emotions arise, don't run from them. Invite them to exist and allow them to inform you, transform you and return you to your natural state of enlightenment.

Quantum physics proves that we are 99.999999999999% space and the physical part of us isn't all that physical. The quantum bits of information that make up our forms are constantly blinking in-and-out of existence. Our physical bodies are constantly being renewed. According to Dr. Deepak Chopra, author, public speaker and alternative medicine advocate, in his novel, *Quantum Healing: Exploring the Frontiers of Mind Body Medicine*, he notes:

> "Ninety-eight percent of the atoms in your body were not there a year ago. The skeleton that seems so solid was not there three months ago. The configuration of the bone cells remains somewhat constant, but atoms of all kinds pass freely back and forth through the cell walls, and by that means you acquire a new skeleton every three months. The skin is new every month. You have a new stomach lining every four days, with the actual surface cells that contact food being renewed every five minutes. The cells in the liver turn over very slowly, but new atoms still flow through them, like water in a river course, making a new liver every six weeks. Even within the brain, whose cells are not replaced once they die, the content of carbon, nitrogen, oxygen, and so on is totally different today from a year ago."[12]

---

[12] Deepak Chopra, *Quantum Healing: Exploring the Frontiers of Mind Body Medicine*, (New York: Bantam Books, 2015), Chap. 3: The Sculpture or the River?

With this knowledge, it's clear that we are also not our bodies, but then what is the force that regenerates the body? What is the consciousness, the spaciousness, the nothingness from which we come?

I personally call the emanation from Source: qi. Some call it prana. Others call it God. The label doesn't really matter. What matters isn't really matter at all, but rather the immaterial world that constantly flows into this world to create the temporal forms we see as the grand illusion of a physical reality.

What is Intuition?

When you learn to stop relying on thinking alone to solve your problems and return to sensing the aliveness within you, your intuition naturally arises. Intuition is learning to listen to the messages your higher self is relaying to you through your human vessel, the body. Following your intuition is following the feelings of love, peace and expansion within your form. To not follow your intuition would be to ignore those feelings. Unfortunately, most of us still do this, instead adhering to the never-ending demands of the ego.

The societal indoctrination we've received tells us to turn to the mind when in a crisis, especially an emotional one, but this keeps us stuck in a perpetual loop of pain, confusion, anxiety and stress. To remove all that instantly, you must return to the body.

To learn how to use your intuition, simply start listening to your body when making decisions. If someone asks you to attend an event, what would happen if instead of checking your schedule or going over the myriad reasons why you should attend or not, you simply checked in with how you felt? It's our bodily sensations that allow us to temporarily time travel and give us a sneak peek into the future. If you feel feelings of contraction, nausea or shame, don't go to the event! Your intuition is informing you that you won't have enough energy for the event or something there may be a threat to your safety. If a sensation arises along with a thought, creating a negative emotion, don't go!

This way of moving through life may feel terrifying at first because some of the answers your intuition will tell you will often inconvenience or anger your ego. If you continue to listen to your body and only follow joyful emotions, you'll enter into a state of consciousness where everything seems to flow effortlessly, where miracles appear magically. The truth is that miracles are always available to you. By re-learning to use your intuition you simply enable yourself to see them. Without the addiction of thinking present, you can also feel them. More real magic!

To begin strengthening your intuition right now, say, "Yes," out loud and see how that feels within your body. Now say, "No," out loud and see how that feels. Now think about something that's been confusing you for a while. Inquire about this situation out loud right now. What reaction did your body give you? Did it feel more like a yes or a no? Always follow your yeses, even if they don't make any logical sense to your mind. Your higher self already knows how events are going to unfold. Trust in that wisdom.

Using Intuition

Learning to trust in your intuition can take extreme patience and persistence, especially if you tend to favour your logical mind or ego over your feelings and emotions. Choosing to follow your intuition may actually cause some guilt at first. If you feel shame after rejecting invitations because your body is telling you that you're too tired to go out, you're not alone. The shame you experience is only a by-product of an attachment to ego, to a story of how things should go. What if you dropped all expectations of what should happen in your life and instead decided only to follow feelings of expansion and bliss? Yes, you would disappoint people, but disappointment is inevitable.

Following your intuition will inconvenience the ego constantly, but it will also allow peace, joy and true satisfaction to surface. By following the feelings of bliss created from within, you create space in your body for higher dimensional information to flow in and through you. This free flow of Source energy allows you to remain energized, inspired and liberated from fear. When you focus on your feelings rather than listen solely to the demands of the mind, you're able to witness the miracles occurring all around you. Without the veil of ego clouding your perception, you begin to move gracefully through life, only choosing that which serves your highest good. In doing this, you allow the highest version of yourself to be brought forth into this world. Without the stagnancy of constant internal chatter, Source consciousness is able to move through you in whatever form feels best in the moment. This surrender into joy enables you to dance through life effortlessly, enabling you to remain present and send love to anything that arises.

With the use of intuition it becomes clear that your mind is not responsible for the outcome of your life. You see that by trusting in the knowledge contained within your body, being sent into your form from your higher self, that life can be as simple and beautiful as you want it to be. By choosing to only follow your bliss in each moment, you float easily through the river of life, rather than battle upstream.

When you have the courage to let go and surrender to the force of love that wants to flow through your form, your internal world is cleansed. Your qi is strengthened and energetic blocks are naturally released. This internal cleansing creates more abundance, security and creativity in your life. You feel your connection to the divine and are able to express it uninhibitedly. Innate psychic gifts often arise with the simple act of listening to the body.

Yes, it can feel terrifying to let go of the mind, to not know what's going to happen next, but doing this will free you from suffering, as the mind will always turn to negativity to continue to have something to chew on. Truth must be experienced and felt. The mind will tempt you with possible outcomes for an imaginary future, but they're just that: possibilities. Life is a grand mystery and none of us have it all figured out. If you can relax into the feeling of not knowing and feel okay with that, suffering will cease.

You don't have to know what's going to happen in order to feel safe. The only thing you have to do is focus on remaining present, on surviving each moment. If something is destined to occur, it will. Worrying will only block Source energy from flowing through you and manifesting miracles.

In the higher dimensions that we all come from, we can already do everything we yearn to do as humans. We came here to experience limitation, so why not enjoy it? Everything has already occurred anyway, so why bother worrying about anything at all?

Anxiety vs. Excitement

It's important to address the difference between excitement and anxiety, because the two are often confused for one another. It's common to feel a little nervous energy when doing something completely new. It's your body's natural response to new stimuli, a defense mechanism. This often arises as sweaty palms, a quicker heartbeat, butterflies in the stomach, a dry mouth, etc. When nervous energy arises, slow down and breathe through it. Usually it will pass. Don't let nerves stop you from going for your dreams. People who remain comfortable don't evolve. Pain propels us forward. We do more as humans to avoid pain than we do to get pleasure, so a little bit of pain can be healthy. If the anxiety doesn't pass and continues to cause you discomfort, you can then discern that your body is warning you against something. If you continually get a pang of discomfort in your gut, for example, trust that your body is telling you, "Stop."

The cells within the enteric system are instinctual and often can be trusted more than the mind, which tends to over think. When trying to discern between anxiety and excitement, first slow down and return to your breath. Sit up straight. Because your own negative thoughts can create anxiety within your body, it's important to observe if it is indeed you who is creating the visceral response, the butterflies in the stomach, the anxiety that sometimes feels like excitement. If you realize that your thoughts are in alignment with your heart and you find that you're still feeling contracted, you can take that as a certain warning from your higher self to choose something else.

It takes practice to discover where your anxiety is coming from, but with slow deep breaths, the truth is always revealed.

PART 4

Heal Emotional Blockages

Negative Emotions are Not Bad

Since childhood most of us were told to supress our negative emotions. If you've spent any time in meditation, it becomes very apparent whether you've been stuffing your shadow-side into the depths of your body. All that stuffing usually results in the blocked root chakra that most people, at least in the Western world, currently suffer from. We walk around with our heads filled with good ideas about what we're going to do in some imaginary future, but have no grounding, no connection to the Earth. This blockage manifests as a feeling of lack; lack of income and lack of meaningful relationships.

It's this suppression and distortion of your energy field that often results in an unbalanced emotional body. Dis-ease is never something that occurs randomly. Any disharmony within the body, including chronic illness, is always the result of poor nutrition, stress, too many toxins, the storing of negative emotions and unprocessed karma (trauma).

If you're currently attaching to a painful memory from your past as a way to create an identity, you may be unconsciously choosing to stay in victimhood. It's not that there's anything wrong with being a victim of the pain of your past or your current circumstance, or even the fear of an unknown future. You can live your entire life blaming other people for any negative experience or emotion that arises in your reality. But what does this actually do? This constant scapegoating continues to keep you in a state of perpetual purgatory, where life is bearable, but there always seems to be something lacking. The thing that is lacking is of course the true bliss that comes with the courage to face your demons and no longer run from them. When you choose to stop running from your problems, or pawning them off on the world around you, something miraculous happens: you see that you in fact are the one choosing to stay in a state of fear, of lack and separation by ignoring your pain.

When you choose to view painful emotions or situations as problematic, life turns into a constant arduous journey uphill. Have you ever made a mistake and felt extremely shameful about it? Afterwards did you perhaps punish yourself even further with self-degradation or thoughts of unworthiness: *I'm a horrible person. I don't deserve to be happy. Nobody will love me.* This all-too-common cycle of self-inflicted pain doesn't help release the pain at all, and instead keeps you trapped within the confines of an inferior ego that learns to feed off your own supply of fear. An inferior ego that believes it is bad or worse than others is just as volatile as an inflated ego.

Face Your Fear

The easiest way to shift into a higher state of consciousness, to release the grip the ego seems to have over your life, is to enter deeply into your own body. Through the simple act of sitting and being with your pain, a transformation starts to occur. You see that any discord in your external reality is a manifestation of the disharmony within you, the result of you choosing to run from your pain.

Though sitting in meditation may be extremely uncomfortable at first, I encourage you to practice the art of surrender. When we choose to step out of our minds temporarily and consciously choose to *be* without the need to do anything, we allow the light of our true essence to emerge from within. It's this light that illuminates the shadow aspects we've hidden for so long.

If you've made living in your mind your usual way of being, it may be quite strange to sit and explore your inner universe. It may even be challenging to feel that you have a body at all! A full body scan is a useful exercise to begin to reconnect to the sensations within you.

Sit quietly and comfortably with your eyes closed and begin to sense the breath. Then begin to notice the subtle energy inside your body. Start at your head. If you're holding any tension in your scalp, forehead, cheeks, lips, etc., let it go. Work your way down through your neck, into your arms, fingers, torso, back, groin, thighs, knees, shins, feet and toes, going as slowly as you need to. Once your whole body is feeling relaxed, observe without judgment any feelings, sensations or thoughts that arise. Don't attach to any emotion or thought. Let them arise and you'll soon see that any uncomfortable sensations dissipate with awareness. This observation of what *is* happening rather than what the mind *thinks* is happening allows any supressed negative emotions to surface and transform back into the peace from which they came. By simply sitting and sensing the breath and allowing all to be exactly as it is, you release yourself from the death grip of the ego and the unconscious cycle of the projection of pain. You see that it's not something outside of you causing any pain, but rather you choosing to supress or project it. When you choose to sit with your pain, it no longer has any power over you. It becomes a sensation that no longer can hurt you.

With a regular practice of watching the process of a negative emotion such as anger within you, it becomes much easier to stop being unconsciously ruled by it. You see that when anger arises, the breath becomes agitated or uneven and tension begins to manifest within the body. When this happens to an untrained mind, the first response is to blame the external for the pain. An experienced meditator knows that all arises from within, begins to watch the uneven breath, and sends love and awareness to any tension. Soon the anger dissipates and no one is harmed.

It's a choice now to step out of victim mentality, to consciously choose to stay present by witnessing the breath and the body. With a regular practice of meditation, staying present becomes your natural way of being. You see that no matter what transpires in your experience, you're able to face it calmly and send any event peace, love and compassion. No longer pulled by the changing vicissitudes of life, you move gracefully through this world, a peaceful warrior, connected to Source consciousness.

An Addiction to Pain

Sometimes the unconscious desire to feed the inferior ego turns into an addiction. The inferior ego begins to crave conflict and seeks it wherever it goes. It knows that it can live just a little longer if there's negative energy to feed off of. It becomes like an entity within you that never has your best interest at heart. In fact, the idea of you choosing to surrender to the moment and let go of it for good terrifies it, for that act would kill it, so it seeks to keep itself alive by causing drama wherever it goes. This constant feeding of the ego with negative thoughts and emotions causes a physical reaction to occur within the brain.

The hormone epinephrine, produced by the adrenal gland, is released when you experience anger, fear or other forms of stress. Increased blood pressure, sweating and pupil dilation are signs that the chemical is being released. The neurotransmitter norepinephrine can also be released from the adrenal medulla and is related to the alertness that some people call an adrenaline rush. The constriction of blood vessels, the contraction of heart muscles, and the dilation of the lungs indicate that the chemical is being released. Both epinephrine and norepinephrine are experienced like an amphetamine and an analgesic in that they provide you with a surge of energy while numbing your pain.

While anger can be useful to help spur you into action, you can actually become addicted to it for energy or motivation. If you've ever felt the need to throw a fit before sitting down to do hours of monotonous work, you've most likely unconsciously given yourself a small dose of pain medication to cope. This method gives you the energy to complete tasks, but often your performance will be subpar.

Getting angry to numb chronic pain, whether physical or emotional is also very common. If you're in a new situation and a sudden burst of social anxiety arises, you may find yourself getting a little angry in order to feel a sense of protection; your energy surges so you can take on whatever arises while your pain subsides momentarily.

You may also be using anger to pull you out of a low emotional state. If you suffer from bouts of depression you're likely to have low norepinephrine levels, so bursts of anger can help motivate you, but this creates a permanent low emotional state where you rely on your anger to fuel action. While this solves momentary problems, inevitably attaching to anger causes blockages within the emotional body and manifests as dis-ease.

The energetic addiction to anger can turn into a physical drug dependency where extremely toxic states become commonplace. To the inferior ego, staying in a painful situation becomes quite comfortable. Of course, if you're unaware that you have been unconsciously operating from a place of lack, the fear that arises with the thought of change can not only seem real but can feel real. When fear arises, the epinephrine can be so deliciously inviting, that you actually begin to choose fear over more peaceful emotions.

Fear arises when you're about to do something dangerous that might hurt your physical form. It's a self-preservation mechanism, but ultimately the real you can never get hurt and can never die. Only your temporary physical form can be damaged, but this never has any effect on your soul.

Fear arises so we have something to triumph over. It keeps us centred and lets us know that we're growing. The contrast fear provides us with enables us to feel grateful after it leaves. In essence, fear is a beautiful gift. There's a big difference between the fear you feel that comes after thinking and the natural fear that appears when you're doing something new. If you're not feeling any natural fear, this means you're not pushing yourself to grow. If you place too much importance on being comfortable, you won't develop. True growth of any kind occurs when you realize that your struggle, your contribution, your divine expression is more important than remaining comfortable.

To release the grip the inferior ego has on you, the first step is to take responsibility for your life. When you choose to step out of victim mentality, something quite spectacular occurs: you reclaim your power and fear no longer has any control over you. If you realize that you've been living under the spell of ego for years, this shift in awareness won't always be so pleasant.

The fear that arises when you choose to stop projecting out your pain onto others with words or outbursts of negative emotion comes from your dying ego. Embrace it and be set free.

Healing the Emotional Body with Chinese Medicine

Traditional Chinese medicine views the body as a holistic system where the organs are associated to specific elements and emotions. You can use this system to address where certain emotional blockages are in your body in order to release them.

Generating relationships can be understood as the mother-son relationships, where the mother gives birth to the son and feeds the son. There are five mother-son relationships within the five elements: wood generates fire, fire generates earth, earth generates metal, metal generates water and water generates wood. When you apply these relationships to the body, a healthy mother organ will naturally nourish the son organ. A healthy liver (wood element) with free-flowing qi will nourish the heart (fire element). A healthy heart will nourish the spleen (earth element). A healthy spleen will nourish the lungs (metal element). Healthy lungs will nourish the kidneys (water element). Healthy kidneys will nourish the liver (wood element).

Healing the Liver

The liver is located in the right upper abdomen underneath the diaphragm and is mainly responsible for filtering blood coming from the digestive tract before sending it to the rest of the body. The liver detoxifies chemicals and metabolizes drugs. It also secretes bile and makes proteins involved in blood clotting. A healthy liver helps to maintain qi flow and allows you to feel happy, calm and balanced. It assists the spleen in sending food and water up while supporting the stomach in sending food down. It's a major organ in helping to maintain the free flow of qi throughout the body to prevent blood and qi stagnation. The liver also controls the function of the tendons and nails. It plays a major role in our eyesight as the liver and eyes are connected through an energy meridian.

A liver that isn't storing and maintaining qi and blood properly can manifest as: blurred vision, night blindness, spasms of the tendons, stoppage of the menstrual cycle, depression, anxiety, anger, irritability, impatience, agitation, headaches, dizziness or paranoia. A liver that isn't helping the digestion and absorption process can manifest as: a lack of appetite, indigestion, diarrhea, constipation or a bitter taste in the mouth. Without proper qi and blood flow, other conditions can manifest: pain in the breasts or upper abdomen, soft or brittle nails, slower movements of the joints or extremities or tremors in the hands and feet.

5Ɖ Healing Technique to Heal the Liver

PART 1:

Get into a relaxed, meditative state where you feel comfortable and safe. Close your eyes and place one hand on your liver and one hand just beneath your navel. Breathe in-and-out through your nose if you can. Focus all your attention on your liver and allow whatever images to arise in your mind's eye to arise. You may see beautiful colours or nature scenes if your liver is healthy. If your liver is in need of extra love, less attractive colours or scenes may arise. What does your liver feel like to you? Is it balanced, happy and comfortable or is there pain and contraction there? If, upon inquiry, you only see beautiful images arise and feel free flowing energy, move onto the next portion of this exercise. If you notice any stagnation of energy or abnormality, focus on it. Ask your liver to speak honestly and freely through you now. Some questions to ask are:

- What's wrong?
- Why are you upset?
- Why are you in pain?
- How have I abused you in any way?
- What do you need to feel better?
- How do you want me to treat you?
- Is there anything I can do to make you happy?
- What do you want?
- How would you feel if you got what you wanted?

Ask your liver any question you feel intuitively drawn to ask and speak aloud any answer that naturally wants to arise. This pure honesty is healing in itself and will often help stagnant energy start to flow again. Focus on the positive emotion your liver would feel if it got what it wanted. Now ask yourself how you would feel if you, too, felt that positive emotion. What kind of activities would you be doing? What would your life look like? Take in a deep breath and send that positive emotion into your liver, along with any positive images or colours that arise. Allow the positive images and emotion to completely fill your liver, forcing the old undesirable or less attractive scenes to completely be absorbed in the new energy you're sending. On the outbreath, the new positive emotion and colours/images grow brighter, stronger and more powerful. You see your liver glow with health and peace. Do this as many times as you need to until the old images or emotions are completely absorbed into the new energy and they no longer exist.

This is an intuitive practice. If you see a pit filled with black tar, you may choose to send green light directly into the pit until it overflows with health once more. There are no limits within this healing technique.

PART 2:

When your liver is radiating with positive energy, with your eyes closed and your hands in the same position, focus your attention on your liver and take in a deep breath. As you breathe, send the breath into your liver while imagining green light entering it, permeating it with healing energy. Then repeat, "Liver, I command you now as God to heal." Exhale and watch your liver glow with green healing energy. Inhale and repeat, "Liver,

I command you now as God to regulate blood and qi flow with ease and to heal my gallbladder." On your next inhale, repeat, "Liver, I command you now as God to heal my eyes, so I may see clearly and be constantly inspired by the beauty of this world." Breathe out and watch your liver grow even brighter. Inhale and repeat, "Liver, I command you now as God to heal my tendons and nails, so I may move gracefully through this world." Breathe out and watch your liver glow. Inhale and repeat, "Liver, I command you now as God to heal and to transmute any anger into patience, peace and harmony." Breathe out and watch your liver glow even brighter. On your inhale, repeat, "I'm sorry for any damage I've caused you. Please forgive me for any mistakes I have made. Thank you from the bottom of my heart. I love you with all my soul."

Continue to place your attention on your glowing green liver as you breathe naturally. If you feel drawn to apologize for any past actions or offer any words of encouragement to your liver, do so now. Then repeat, "It's okay that you're here. You have a right to be here. You are worthy of being here. I love you." When you're ready, send the green light concentrated in your liver to your entire body. Place your awareness on your entire form now and repeat, "It's okay that you're here. You have a right to be here. You are worthy of being here. I love you." On another outbreath, send the healing energy out into the room and beyond into the universe and repeat, "It's okay that you're here. You have a right to be here. You are worthy of being here. I love you."

When you're ready, open your eyes and return to your normal state of consciousness.

Healing the Spleen:

The spleen is located in the left upper abdomen, to the left of the stomach. A healthy spleen filters blood as a part of the immune system. Old red blood cells are recycled in the spleen and platelets and white blood cells are stored there. The spleen helps fight bacteria that cause pneumonia and meningitis while producing qi for the whole body. A healthy spleen transports, distributes, transforms and absorbs food and water. It transports liquids to the lungs and divides the liquids into clear and unclear. The unclear liquids are transformed into perspiration, urine or stool, and excreted. The spleen also helps create a healthy appetite, a sense of taste and pink lips while helping to maintain strong muscles.

A spleen that has difficulties in transporting, distributing or transforming food can manifest as: poor appetite, indigestion, bowel issues, weight loss, water retention or diarrhea. When the spleen isn't producing strong qi and blood, this can manifest as: blood in the stool or urine or hemorrhaging. Stagnant qi in the spleen can manifest as: poor appetite, a lack of taste or a feeling of fullness in the upper abdomen. Weak or depleted qi in the spleen can manifest as: weak muscles or extremities.

5D Healing Technique to Heal the Spleen

PART 1:

Repeat the instructions in Part 1 from the **5D Healing Technique to Heal the Liver**, but instead, focus on your spleen. Place one hand on your navel and the other on your spleen. You can choose to breathe gold light into your spleen to nourish it.

PART 2:

When your spleen is radiating with positive energy, with your eyes closed and your hands in the same position, focus your attention on your spleen and take in a deep breath. As you breathe, send the breath into your spleen while imagining gold light entering it, permeating it with healing energy. Then repeat, "Spleen, I command you now as God to heal." Exhale and watch your spleen glow with gold healing energy. Inhale and repeat, "Spleen, I command you now as God to absorb food and water easily and to transform any worry into compassion." On your next inhale, breathe in gold light and repeat, "Spleen, I command you now as God to strengthen my muscles and limbs, so I may walk confidently through this world." Breathe out and watch your spleen grow even brighter. Inhale and repeat, "Spleen, I command you now as God to heal my lips, mouth, gums and teeth so I may speak from my highest divine authority and only offer words of love, encouragement and compassion." Breathe out and watch your spleen glow. On your inhale, repeat, "Spleen, I command you now as God to strengthen my qi and heal my stomach, so I may exist with radiant health and only offer the highest love into this world." Breathe out, watch your spleen glow even brighter. Inhale and repeat, "I'm sorry for any damage I've caused you. Please forgive me for any mistakes I have made. Thank you from the bottom of my heart. I love you with all my soul."

Continue to place your attention on your glowing gold spleen as you breathe naturally. If you feel drawn to apologize for any past actions or offer any words of encouragement to your spleen, do so now. Then repeat, "It's okay that you're here. You have a right to be here. You are worthy of being here. I love you." When you're ready, send the gold light concentrated in your spleen to your entire body. Place your awareness on your entire form now and repeat, "It's okay that you're here. You have a right to be here. You are worthy of being here. I love you." On another outbreath, send the healing energy out into the room and beyond into the universe and repeat, "It's okay that you're here. You have a right to be here. You are worthy of being here. I love you."

When you're ready, open your eyes and return to your normal state of consciousness.

Healing the Lungs

The lungs are located in the thoracic cavity of the chest, one on the left and another on the right. The lungs allow you to take in oxygen and exhale carbon dioxide. The lungs help to form zong qi (gathering qi). Zong qi is formed by the inhalation of fresh air in combination with the food essence sent by the spleen. Zong qi is sent up by the spleen to the larynx where it gives strength to the voice. The lungs are the primary organ responsible for nourishing the skin and hair along with transporting liquid to the kidneys and urinary bladder. This creates normal water metabolism.

Lungs that are deficient in qi could lead to respiratory disorders, breathing difficulties, asthma, coughing or fatigue. If the nose is obstructed, a stuffy or runny nose can manifest. If there is not enough zong qi being created through the act of combining inhaled air and food essence, shortness of breath, exhaustion or a weak voice can manifest. If there is a dysfunction of the lung qi and imbalance of water metabolism, lack of urine or painful urine can manifest. If qi in the lungs cannot flow downward, skin can appear sallow, pale or dry.

5D Healing Technique to Heal the Lungs

PART 1:

Repeat the instructions in Part 1 from the **5D Healing Technique to Heal the Liver**, but instead, focus on your lungs. Place one hand on your navel and the other on your lungs. You can choose to breathe white light into your lungs to nourish them.

PART 2:

When your lungs are radiating with positive energy, with your eyes closed and your hands in the same position, focus your attention on your lungs and take in a deep breath. As you breathe, send the breath into your lungs while imagining white light entering them, permeating them with healing energy. Then repeat, "Lungs, I command you now as God to heal." Exhale and watch your lungs glow with white healing energy. Inhale and repeat, "Lungs,

I command you now as God to heal my large intestine and to generate powerful qi." Exhale and then take in another white light breath and repeat, "Lungs, I command you now as God to send food essences and liquids to nourish my entire body, so I may walk through life strong and empowered." Breathe out and watch your lungs grow even brighter. Inhale and repeat, "Lungs, I command you now as God to create a perfect metabolism and to transmute any sadness into courage." Breathe out and watch your lungs glow. Inhale and then repeat, "Lungs, I command you now as God to create perfect nose and breathing functions, so I may breathe easily and speak and sing from my highest divine authority, only offering love into this world." Breathe out, watch your lungs glow even brighter. Inhale and repeat, "I'm sorry for any damage I've caused you. Please forgive me for any mistakes I have made. Thank you from the bottom of my heart. I love you with all my soul."

Continue to place your attention on your glowing white lungs as you breathe naturally. If you feel drawn to apologize for any past actions or offer any words of encouragement to your lungs, do so now. Then repeat, "It's okay that you're here. You have a right to be here. You are worthy of being here. I love you." When you're ready, send the white light concentrated in your lungs to your entire body. Place your awareness on your entire form now and repeat, "It's okay that you're here. You have a right to be here. You are worthy of being here. I love you." On another outbreath, send the healing energy out into the room and beyond into the universe and repeat, "It's okay that you're here. You have a right to be here. You are worthy of being here. I love you."

When you're ready, open your eyes and return to your normal state of consciousness.

Healing the Kidneys

The kidneys are located in the back of the abdomen on either side of the spinal column. The inherited essence of life (qi) from your parents is stored within the kidneys both before and after birth. The essence of life in the kidneys is transformed into bone marrow which creates healthy bones and teeth. The kidneys support the lungs with the inhalation of air and create strong and clear hearing. With the addition of food, the stored qi in the kidneys works to help the body grow, develop and reproduce. The kidneys help maintain a proper balance of fluids and sustain water circulation in the body. Body fluid with the nourishment from food gets sent to all the major organs in the body.

The stored qi in the kidneys gets sent to all the major organs and any excess gets stored within the kidneys for later use. If the organs are depleted of vital energy, the kidneys will send their stored essence to the organs and sensations of heat in the chest, palms or soles of the feet may arise, along with night sweats, cold or pain in the lumbar spine area and knees or even infertility. If there are blockages in water metabolism, irregular urination could result. Since the kidneys support the lungs, imbalances within them can result in breathing difficulties. A lack of kidney qi can manifest as: weak bones, hair or teeth, along with baldness or grey hair. Loss of hearing, sensitivity to sounds, constipation, impotence or diarrhea can also manifest.

5D Healing Technique to Heal the Kidneys

PART 1:

Repeat the instructions in Part 1 from the **5D Healing Technique to Heal the Liver**, but instead, focus on your kidneys. Place one hand on your navel and the other on your kidneys. You can choose to breathe blue light into your kidneys to nourish them.

PART 2:

When your kidneys are radiating with positive energy, with your eyes closed and your hands in the same position, focus your attention on your kidneys and take in a deep breath. As you breathe, send the breath into your kidneys while imagining blue light entering them, permeating them with healing energy. Then repeat, "Kidneys, I command you now as God to heal." Exhale and watch your kidneys glow with blue healing energy. Inhale and repeat, "Kidneys, I command you now as God to heal my urinary bladder and to create strong kidney jing and qi." Exhale and then take in another blue light breath. Repeat, "Kidneys, I command you now as God to create perfect water metabolism and to transmute any fear within me into calmness and love." Breathe out and watch your kidneys grow even brighter. Inhale and then repeat, "Kidneys, I command you now as God to make my bones, bone marrow, teeth and hair strong and healthy." Breathe out and watch your kidneys and lungs glow. Inhale and repeat, "Kidneys, I command you now as God to hear clearly and to have perfect elimination." Breathe out, watch your kidneys glow even brighter. Inhale and repeat, "I'm sorry for any damage

I've caused you. Please forgive me for any mistakes I have made. Thank you from the bottom of my heart. I love you with all my soul."

Continue to place your attention on your glowing blue kidneys as you breathe naturally. If you feel drawn to apologize for any past actions or offer any words of encouragement to your kidneys, do so now. Then repeat, "It's okay that you're here. You have a right to be here. You are worthy of being here. I love you." When you're ready, send the blue light concentrated in your kidneys to your entire body. Place your awareness on your entire form now and repeat, "It's okay that you're here. You have a right to be here. You are worthy of being here. I love you." On another outbreath, send the healing energy out into the room and beyond into the universe and repeat, "It's okay that you're here. You have a right to be here. You are worthy of being here. I love you."

When you're ready, open your eyes and return to your normal state of consciousness.

Healing the Heart

The heart is located in the left chest and is surrounded by a protective sac called the pericardium. The heart circulates blood throughout the entire body and when beating regularly, helps us to maintain a balanced, calm and peaceful mood. The heart is connected to the sense of taste and creates a healthy pink, moist and free-moving tongue. Normal perspiration is also a sign of a healthy heart.

A lack of blood in the heart can manifest as a weak pulse or irregular heartbeat. A lack of circulation produces a pale complexion and a weak pulse. An irregular heartbeat can manifest as: mental disorder, insomnia, palpitations or depression. A pale, red, dark or purple tongue can also manifest along with the inability to speak. Excessive perspiration can also be a sign of an unbalanced heart.

5D Healing Technique to Heal the Heart

PART 1:

Repeat the instructions in Part 1 from the **5D Healing Technique to Heal the Liver**, but instead, focus on your heart. Place one hand on your navel and the other on your heart. You can choose to breathe red light into your heart to nourish it.

PART 2:

When your heart is radiating with positive energy, with your eyes closed and your hands in the same position, focus your attention on your heart and take in a deep breath. As you breathe, send the breath into your heart while imagining red light entering it, permeating it with healing energy. Then repeat, "Heart, I command you now as God to heal." Exhale and watch your heart glow with red healing energy. Inhale and repeat, "Heart, I command you now as God to circulate blood perfectly and to transmute any depression or anxiety into joy." Exhale and then take in another breath of red light. Repeat, "Heart, I command you now as God to create glowing, clear complexion so I may express true beauty into this world." Breathe out and watch your heart grow even brighter. Inhale and then repeat, "Heart,

I command you now as God to clear my mind so I may only channel thoughts of the highest divine order." Breathe out and watch your heart glow. Inhale and repeat, "Heart, I command you now as God to heal my small intestine and to create a perfect tongue and normal perspiration." Breathe out and watch your heart glow even brighter. Inhale and repeat, "I'm sorry for any damage I've caused you. Please forgive me for any mistakes I have made. Thank you. I love you with all my soul."

Continue to place your attention on your glowing red heart as you breathe naturally. If you feel drawn to apologize for any past actions or offer any words of encouragement to your heart, do so now. Then repeat, "It's okay that you're here. You have a right to be here. You are worthy of being here. I love you." When you're ready, send the red light concentrated in your heart to your entire body. Place your awareness on your entire form now and repeat, "It's okay that you're here. You have a right to be here. You are worthy of being here. I love you." On another outbreath, send the healing energy out into the room and beyond into the universe and repeat, "It's okay that you're here. You have a right to be here. You are worthy of being here. I love you."

When you're ready, open your eyes and return to your normal state of consciousness.

5D Healing Technique: Energetic Organ Cleanse

If you don't have a lot of time to enter into a long meditation, you can use this technique to quickly find peace and release toxic energy from your organs.

1. Get into a meditative state by slowing your breath and closing your eyes.

2. Place your hands on your liver. Send green light and breath through your crown chakra, down through your hands, and into your liver. Continue to imagine spiritual energy entering your liver and repeat, "I draw my fifth dimensional self into my body to heal me. I transmute this anger to love throughout all densities, dimensions, time and space, and so it is."

3. Place your hands on your spleen. Send gold light and breath through your crown chakra, down through your hands into your spleen. Continue to imagine spiritual energy entering your spleen and repeat, "I draw my fifth dimensional self into my body to heal me. I transmute this worry to love throughout all densities, dimensions, time and space, and so it is."

4. Place your hands on your lungs. Send white light and breath through your crown chakra, down through your hands, and into your lungs. Continue to imagine spiritual energy entering your lungs and repeat, "I draw my fifth dimensional self into my body to heal me. I transmute this shame to love throughout all densities, dimensions, time and space, and so it is."

5. Place your hands on your kidneys. Send blue light and breath through your crown chakra, down through your hands, and into your kidneys. Continue to imagine spiritual energy entering your kidneys and repeat, "I draw my fifth dimensional self into my body to heal me. I transmute this fear to love throughout all densities, dimensions, time and space, and so it is."

6. Place your hands on your heart. Send red light and breath through your crown chakra, down through your hands, into your heart. Continue to imagine spiritual energy entering your

heart and repeat, "I draw my fifth dimensional self into my body to heal me. I transmute this anxiety to love throughout all densities, dimensions, time and space, and so it is."

Offer a prayer of thanks to your guides and angels and to Source if you wish. Open your eyes and continue with your day, balanced and renewed.

Practical Spiritual Healing

"Many spiritual practitioners note that sitting in observance of our emotional pain is a catalyst for healing it. However, few delineate a clear methodology for this practice. Christina's Fifth Dimensional Healing method provides a practical outline for engaging emotional pain. What's more impressive is its simplicity. Spiritual fluff has been curbed in favor of real world steps that are easy-to-remember and activate whenever challenging circumstances enter one's experience. This is especially valuable for modern lifestyles that find allocating time for one's spiritual well-being to be a precious commodity."

Mike Riddick, Author

Fifth Dimensional Healing Technique: Chakra Cleanse

This is a simple exercise that you can do to quickly clear your chakras and find alignment. Always start from the root chakra and work your way up to the crown chakra.

1. Get into a meditative state by slowing your breath and closing your eyes.

2. Place both hands on your root chakra. Take a deep breath in and imagine red light from Source flowing in through your crown and moving down into your arms. Let the healing light flow out through your hands into your root. Exhale and continue to repeat this visualization process. Repeat out loud, "I draw my fifth dimensional self into my body to heal me. I transmute this instability into stability, abundance and strength throughout all densities, dimensions, time and space, and so it is."

3. Place your hands on your sacral chakra. Repeat the breathing and visualization instructions from step two, but instead send orange light through your hands. Repeat out loud, "I draw my fifth dimensional self into my body to heal me. I transmute this stagnancy into creativity, sensuality and flow throughout all densities, dimensions, time and space, and so it is."

4. Place your hands on your solar plexus chakra. Repeat the breathing and visualization instructions from step two, but instead send yellow light through your hands. Repeat out loud, "I draw my fifth dimensional self into my body to heal me. I transmute this fear to express myself into true confidence, passion and divine will throughout all densities, dimensions, time and space, and so it is."

5. Place your hands on your heart chakra. Repeat the breathing and visualization instructions from step two, but instead send green light through your hands. Repeat out loud, "I draw my fifth dimensional self into my body to heal me. I transmute this anxiety into joy, compassion and peace throughout all densities, dimensions, time and space, and so it is."

6. Place your hands on your throat chakra. Repeat the breathing and visualization instructions from step two, but instead send blue light through your hands. Repeat out loud, "I draw my fifth dimensional self into my body to heal me. I transmute this fear to express myself into uninhibited divine expression, song and truth throughout all densities, dimensions, time and space, and so it is."

7. Place your hands on your third eye chakra. Repeat the breathing and visualization instructions from step two, but instead send indigo light through your hands. Repeat out loud, "I draw my fifth dimensional self into my body to heal me. I transmute this unconsciousness into divine consciousness, clarity and wisdom throughout all densities, dimensions, time and space, and so it is."

8. Place your hands on your crown chakra. Repeat the breathing and visualization instructions from step two, but instead send violet light through your hands. Repeat out loud, "I draw my fifth dimensional self into my body to heal me. I transmute this disconnection with Source into sacred union with Source, enlightenment and power throughout all densities, dimensions, time and space, and so it is."

Offer a prayer of thanks to any guides or angels you may have worked with, and to the Source of all. Open your eyes whenever you feel ready and continue your day, renewed and connected to the truth of your being.

Heart Health

With the heightened awareness that comes with the practice of meditation, it becomes clear that any disharmony in your external world is always there to help you return to loving your own heart, your own innocent nature.

If a lover has ever wronged you, think back to the words you said about him/her to a friend. Perhaps you complained that your lover didn't give you enough attention or didn't make enough time for you? Now imagine those words coming from your own heart. What if the external was really only a projection of what was going on inside you? What if it was actually your heart demanding that you send it more attention? Whatever you want someone else to give you, you must give to yourself first.

If you choose to hold onto anger directed at an ex, for example, you'll keep a soul contract alive that will inevitably arise in the form of another person for you to deal with. Why not turn inward and release the anger safely instead?

Close your eyes for a moment and think about someone who triggers you the most. This could be a friend, an ex, a parent, etc. Ask yourself, "What would that person have to say to me in order for me to forgive them?" In meditation, after entering into the theta state, picture your enemy and have him speak the answer to you. If it's uncomfortable for you to look at the person, transform him into a happier version, perhaps when you first met him. Imagining the person as his higher self can work well too. If this is still too painful, simply place your hands over your heart and speak the words aloud or internally. You may find the person saying things such as, "I was wrong. I didn't know I hurt you.

I'm so sorry. I had no idea I hurt you. I'm so sorry I couldn't see you clearly. I'm so sorry I was so selfish and unkind. I was an awful person. I was in the wrong." Don't worry about being kind during this exercise. The more honest you can be, the better. Then, when you're ready to forgive, do so.

When you can truly forgive those who have hurt you, you break outdated soul contracts and release yourself from the trap of continuous toxic relationships. If you're in a toxic relationship right now where you're fighting more than you're loving, stop for a moment to consider what soul contracts you still have. What traumas are you still carrying with you, perhaps from childhood, that are now playing out in your romantic relationships?

If you're angry at a parent who abandoned you in your teenage years and haven't forgiven him/her, expect your lovers to walk out on you exactly the way your parent did. Until you can release the soul contract with that parent internally, life will present you with external opportunities to do so.

Karma = Stored Trauma

Karma is stored trauma within our physical, emotional, mental and energetic bodies, as well as our cells and DNA. This trauma is taken on from our parents, previous lives and the present one. Think about it logically. Let's say you have a mother who was emotionally abused in a previous lifetime. She comes into her next life with that trauma stored deep in her energetic body. Life presents her with "negative" situations to steer her back to her inner world to clear the trauma. If she ignores the warning signs, resists life and continues to blame her external circumstances for her pain, life pushes harder. You, as her child, take on some of that trauma/karma at birth, and as you receive her projections of pain. When you clear your own trauma/karma, you also help to clear your parent's karma by default.

Yes, you chose your parents for a very specific combination of energy in order to facilitate the highest growth within this lifetime. If you were born into a dysfunctional family, think about how your situation has helped you grow and become stronger. How has your trauma transformed you? How can each negative situation be a blessing in disguise? How is your current situation sacred?

Forgiveness Prayer

To practice the art of forgiveness, first think about someone who triggers you to feel intense negative emotions. If no one arises, perhaps you want to forgive yourself? Place your hands on your heart and repeat: "The Source of all that exists, I love you and ask for you from my soul to forgive my ancestors and me for all the mistakes that we have made in all lifetimes. To all the souls who my ancestors and I have hurt, I apologize from my soul. I'm so sorry for the pain I have caused. To any darkness that exists within me, I forgive you and I love you as well. I will offer the highest love unconditionally to all beings to create heaven on Earth. And so it is."

You can invite any darkness within you to be with you during your meditation practice. As you chant or repeat mantras, you will help to purify the darkness so it will leave you safely. Never be afraid of darkness or negative emotions, as they're only distortions of the one consciousness and are still aspects of you that need love.

When you choose to completely forgive yourself and your enemies you are released from the bondage of soul contracts that cause discord in relationships. You remove energetic blockages causing dis-ease and enter into a world free of conflict. When you encounter drama, you meet it with compassion and thank it for returning you to your loving heart space.

Practicing Self-Love

When you release soul contracts and energetic blockages, it becomes much easier to relax and practice the art of self-love. How does one actually love the self and what is the self I am referring to? Being-love would be more appropriate, because loving your body, mind or image alone will never bring you into a state of completion. To connect to the true self, you must turn to the heart, the gateway to the soul. Self-love is learning to love your own heart.

To begin loving your own heart, sit in meditation and talk to your heart. Ask it:

- How do you feel?
- What are your desires?
- What are your aversions?
- What kind of activities do you prefer?
- What kind of activities do you not want to participate in?
- What kind of people do you want to spend time with?
- What kind of people do you want to avoid?
- What kinds of foods do you love?
- What kinds of foods do you want to avoid?

- Is there anything I could be doing more of to make you happy?
- What kind of music do you enjoy?
- What colours do you enjoy?
- What fragrances make you happy?
- What images soothe you?
- What type of touch makes you happy?
- How do you feel most loved?

You can write down your responses or simply let the images come. Once you know what your heart truly desires, make an effort to start living out your heart's desires. A good way to practice true self-love is by taking yourself out on a date.

Think about what kind of activities you would wait to do with a partner. Why not do them with yourself? Take yourself out to a coffee shop and curl up with a hot drink and a good book. Attend a vegan cooking class and learn how to nourish your body with delicious food. Wander around an art gallery dressed to the nines while pretending you're at the Louvre. Go to a yoga class and chant your way into ecstatic bliss.

Without the distraction of another person around, you'll get to know what truly makes you tick and what you truly desire. Without the responsibility of having to remain compassionate toward another soul, you'll get to explore your own, and possibly even discover why you came here in the first place! Who knows, you may actually *like* being with yourself, and the activities you try on your own may score you a few new friends or perhaps a soul mate.

If you learn to become your own best friend and can enjoy spending hours with yourself, then you won't need another person to be happy. You'll feel complete and have genuine love to offer another soul.

Healthy vs. Unhealthy Relationships

In healthy relationships both partners realize that they are sovereign beings, already complete, and come together to exist, grow and play in love. There is no blame or need involved in true loving relationships and definitely no abuse on any level.

If you find yourself in an abusive relationship, communicate your feelings to solve the issue. Ask yourself what your main commitment in life is to. Does it align with your partner's commitment? If not, compromise. If that doesn't work, don't ever be afraid to hurt the other person's feelings by leaving immediately. Sometimes it's difficult to see the bigger picture—what's actually beneficial for your soul—while so entrenched in a romantic relationship. If your partner won't let you take space, you *must* leave, even if temporarily to gain perspective.

Intimate relationships enable us to evolve spiritually. It's natural to get triggered by your partner, but it's not natural to blame, judge or hold onto toxic emotions after an emotional outburst. If your partner gets triggered and starts yelling, slow your breath and simply hold space. Allow your partner to express pain within the safety of your intimate connection. Thank your partner for being brave enough to express pain. Thank yourself for creating a safe space for your partner to heal in. Forgive, let go and move on stronger.

If you're feeling triggered by your partner, instead of lashing out, explain how you're feeling. "I'm feeling upset right now," is a much more powerful statement than, "You're making me upset." If you need space, express it. If you need affection, express it.

In a loving, harmonious relationship, where each person compromises, there is always room to hold space. Telling the triggered person why they are wrong or trying to fix him while he's still processing pain is futile, childish and extremely unempathetic. Allow the triggered person to release and return to love.

Twin Flames

A lot of toxic relationships start off as intensely passionate ones where both people cannot stop thinking about each other and feel that they need each other to exist. This feels a lot like love, but in fact, it's toxic and codependent. These fiery romances are usually twin flame connections where two people with unresolved traumas come together, attracted to each other's pain. Upon triggering each other, the pain can sometimes make the relationship seem more exciting, dramatic or meaningful, but once again, this isn't love. These romances are destined to fail. How can someone you love turn into someone you despise? Because it was never love in the first place, only an attraction to pain in order to remove trauma/karma.

When twin flames come together, they usually mirror the best and very worst qualities of each other. Every negative habit a person has been supressing is revealed and it's not a pretty sight to behold. Raging battles, name calling and finger pointing often ensue as neither party can see the other person clearly, distracted by pain. The truth is they're not meant to resolve each other's conflict. They're meant to split again to continue the healing work on their own. Twin flames act as catalysts for each other, igniting the deepest passion and then quickly burning out and fading away. The scars from the fire are often very painful, but they too heal in time.

You will draw twin flame relationships to you if you are neglecting your own heart and looking outside yourself for acceptance or approval. The funny thing is that some of the most horrible relationships on Earth are actually with close soul group members. Our enemies are usually our best companions in the higher realms and thus know us the best and can trigger us like no other. Though painful, they spur us into action to help us realign with our true soul path.

⊱⊰

When Self-Love Feels Silly

Learning to love your own heart takes a bit of persistence, especially since we've all been so conditioned to only appreciate the love we receive from others. If it's uncomfortable for you to receive at all, you are definitely not alone! After years of media brainwashing telling you that you're an incomplete being that needs to make itself better with products in order to be worthy of love, it's going to take some practice.

If telling yourself, "I love you," feels uncomfortable at first, that's okay. Continue to say it to yourself until it feels real. A good exercise is to look into your own eyes in the mirror. Once you're gazing at your own reflection say, "I love you." If any limiting thoughts arise, question them until you find their source. Take away their power and continue to send yourself love.

Deep in meditation, when you're producing theta brain waves, tell yourself the compliments you would want to hear from a lover: "You're beautiful. You're sexy. You're so smart. You're hilarious!

You're the most amazing person I've ever met." Whatever you want someone to say to you, say it to your own heart. In the theta state, you'll be accessing your subconscious mind which doesn't know the difference between you or another person talking.

Soul Mates

Once you're comfortable receiving love completely, you'll be able to offer it freely. You won't have to search for your soul mate. He/she will arise naturally when you love your own heart completely. The only searching that you'll have to do is within. Once you discover who you truly are and what you truly desire, your dream lover will manifest. It will seem effortless and easy.

In a true soul mate relationship, you feel comfortable around your partner as he's an accurate reflection of your healed heart. There is no desire to manipulate or fix the other person. Instead, there is only a curiosity to get to know the other person's soul on a deeper level.

Just as you can have many twin flame relationships, you can also have many soul mate relationships. Two souls come together for a specific purpose, often to help each other grow or to empower each other to create. Once the learning is over, the souls part. For some, the connection lasts lifetimes. For others, a few years or less. In the grander perspective, we are all of one consciousness and the concept of needing another soul to be happy is absurd. We see that in truth we are always with our beloved ones, connected to all souls through the vast field of awareness that permeates all things. There is no loneliness when you return to the truth of your being, only trust and appreciation for what arises. However, our human perspective is one of opposites which seeks to unite with others to feel whole. There is no shame in desiring connection for it does indeed remind us of our true unified nature. Our challenge and gift is to remain present while in the presence of others.

Sacred Sex

Relationships can be a vehicle for learning, transformation and ultimately connecting to the divine. Intercourse can be used to connect to your partner on the deepest level and in doing so: connect to God. By surrendering fully to the moment as you make love, you transcend the mind, the heart and even the body to merge with the divine.

Tantra, a Sanskrit word that means *woven together* is a wonderful way to deepen your level of intimacy with yourself, your partner and God. Tantra is an ancient Hindu energy practice designed to help people channel God's energy into their forms. Below are some sexual Tantric practices that you can explore with a partner. You may also choose to modify the exercises to perform them solo:

1. Synch your chakras: Sit across from your partner and wrap your legs around him/her. Stare into your partner's eyes and synchronize your breathing. You can choose to hold hands if that feels comfortable. Begin by making orgasmic sounds which can include moans or even funny sounds such as animal growls. If you start laughing, great! Laughter will raise your emotional state and open your heart. Have one person begin by breathing out and sending red light from his/her root chakra into the other person's root chakra. The receiver should breathe in when receiving. The breaths will no longer be synched. Once the red light is received, the

receiver then breathes out the red light into the partner's root chakra. The partner breathes in the light and repeats for a total of three exchanges. Repeat the process by exchanging coloured light up through the chakras until you reach the crown. This exercise is especially beneficial for people who are energetically sensitive or who have a hard time grounding into their bodies. If you've experienced sexual trauma and find it difficult to relax during sex, this exercise may be helpful for removing unwanted thoughts or emotions that make it difficult to connect.

2. Circulate your energy: Sitting across from one another, one partner begins by sending golden light out through his/her root chakra into the other partner's root chakra. The giver should breathe out as the receiver breathes in. The receiver then pulls the light up to his/her heart chakra and breathes out, sending the light to the partner's heart chakra. The energy is circulated back down to the root and the process begins again. Three full circulations are recommended. The partner who received first can then become the giver for another round of three.

3. Infinite love: You may also choose to practice circulating your energy though these channels on your own. There are two major energy circuits within the body, the divine energy and divine matter circles. The divine energy circle begins at the root chakra and travels up through the chakras to reach the crown. Then it makes its way down in front of the spine back to the root. The divine matter circle begins at the root chakra and makes its way up the tail bone, spine and up to the crown. It moves over the top of the head and travels down through the chakras back to the root.

As I was contemplating these two energy circuits, a Tantric practice was channelled to me. To begin, one person sends golden light through his/her divine energy channel. As she sends the light up the chakras, she inhales. When the light reaches the top of the head and then begins to travel back down, she exhales. She sends the golden light to the other person's root chakra for the partner to begin the same process. After the partner has finished circulating the energy through his divine energy circle, he sends the energy back to the other person. The receiver now circulates the energy through her divine matter circle and sends the energy to the partner to do the same. This sharing of energy creates an infinity symbol, linking both people energetically. It's important to note that the breaths won't be synched for this exercise. When one person breathes out, the other person breathes in. Do three complete cycles, which will create six infinity symbols: 888.

4. Using orgasms to heal: This is one you can try on your own! When you orgasm, instead of clenching your groin or releasing your energy out your feet, relax as much as possible. Take in a deep breath and send your energy up your spine to your head. Send the energy to your third eye and then down into your heart. Once the energy reaches your heart, finish the inhalation. As you finish the breath, set an intention to heal your body. Relax completely and let the orgasmic energy flow into your form. You can even direct the energy to someone else to heal them, or use it to strengthen your manifestations.

Venusian Transmission on True Beauty:

When you choose to become completely sovereign and no longer project your pain onto others, realizing that they are inseparable from your own being, your true essence has a chance to blossom. With a release of toxic emotional energy, especially from the heart, your innocence begins to emerge once more. With a re-emergence of this innocence, beauty arises in its purest form.

Muse now on what you consider to be beautiful. What makes you smile and marvel at the immaculate design of the universe? What evokes emotions buried deep within you, leaves you breathless, immovable, present and forever transformed? The infectious laughter of a child? The masterful song of a bird? What do these have in common you ask? We repeat humbly: innocence.

The innocence we speak of has nothing to do with a lack of intelligence. Rather, it evokes the highest awareness you may witness. It is true that only with a stilling of the mind and a softening of the heart that the power creating the world which you see has a chance to move through you and marvel at its own creation. It is only with a return to witnessing all, with the wonder and curiosity of a child, that true beauty can be seen. In this state of pure fascination for life, you see that all of reality is in fact a creation of the divine, which is very much who you are, dear child. We humbly urge you now to not reserve your appreciation of beauty for specific works of art or obviously innocent creatures. We instead urge you now to witness that everything contains this same innocent nature within and we request that you look for this nature within you and within all. The pure creative potential, pure love that emanates from all things, is readily available for those with eyes to see.

If you do not create the breath that you breathe, are you still responsible for the creation of anything that comes after? Relax into this notion for a moment. Realize deeply that it is not the *you* that you identify with so often that is responsible for the beauty which you create. The beautiful works of art you produce, whether they may come in the form of a song, a meal or even a child, manifest from the divine creator, who of course is also you. This is the part of you which remembers that it is love itself and sees all as a creation of that love, as a manifestation of the divine beauty, power and truth.

How to return to the state of wonder you ask? Merge with the breath being breathed into your temporary human form. Breathe in the spaciousness around you and realize that it is one with spaciousness within. Focus on the emptiness contained within all forms. It is here in the nothingness that you will find God. As you begin to see that God is in all things, you will remember that all is sacred and be able to look upon life with a genuine reverence.

It is with practice that a maintenance of this ever-curious state of innocence may be held. Since it is not your mind, the personality you create to protect yourself, creating this world, you may rest assured that you do not have to force creativity or beauty to arise. With a surrender into the state of presence, every action is transmuted into the sacred play of God being witnessed by you. Every movement, every breath, a masterpiece.

Fear not dear child! The universe is infinitely and divinely intelligent and only requires your complete trust to move miracles through your human vessel! It is in this state of pure presence, witnessing all as the divine through the eyes of the divine, remembering that you indeed created all of this for your enjoyment, that beauty can even be appreciated at all!

Think for a moment. When have your most precious ideas sprung forth? Always from beyond the mind, from the eternal spaciousness, the pure potential that you are.

Forget the societally indoctrinated beliefs about beauty forced upon you from the media. The concept that beauty is merely physical is nonsensical. While yes, the sacred math of the universe does create physical perfection that can be observed with the eyes, this alone does not create true beauty. Your so-called flawlessness is only a by-product of the innocence of which we speak, the pure love of the divine manifested in physical form. The attempts to replicate the physical beauty of the divine without first purifying the soul will only fool the blind ones who look only with the eyes.

Attempting to attract others with physical beauty alone is a form of deceptive and self-serving black magic that will always end in suffering. To focus on the illusion of the physical world and attach to it for a sense of security will keep you blind to the divine beauty within you and all you witness. This impairment may not be obvious at first, but with time will grow unbearable. As beauty is a sacred and necessary part of the human experience, it will be natural for you to search for it, but search not with the mind. Close the eyes and light the fire within. Illuminate the pathway to the heart and there, reside.

It is within the heart that you must dwell, the place where all beauty springs forth from. Search the caverns of your heart and if you come across a curse directed at yourself or another, you must invite this curse to be with you. Question the curse. Why is it so angry? What is its purpose for taking residence within you? What does it require before it leaves? Invite your pain to lunch and listen. What complaints do you carry about those who have betrayed or hurt you? Do you see now, dear one, that any complaint about another is really coming from your innocent heart that longs to be seen, loved and heard by you?

Take in a slow deep breath and place a hand over your heart now. Can you feel the reverberation in your chest, pulsing out into your palm? Can you feel the power, the truth, the perfection already contained within you? Without having to think a single thought, your heart beats on, pumping blood throughout your entire form, energizing you and gifting you with life! Thank your heart now and apologize for ever ignoring it.

"Dear heart, I'm so sorry for not listening to you when you've been speaking to me all this time, doing your best to guide me through life. Please forgive me for not seeing you clearly. Thank you for showing me the truth, for always protecting me. I love you with all my soul."

Realize deeply that the beauty you seek externally is already contained within you and to merge with it fully, to witness it in all its glory, you must set yourself free. Thank your pain, your anger, your guilt and your shame for showing you what you are not, for returning you to the purity, the divine perfection, that you've always been. Cry, release and become still once more.

As you sit with an awareness of your heart beating in your chest, feel that the true beauty you seek is within and now feel that beauty emanating from you, creating all that you see. This dream you call reality is your own beautiful imagination, bursting forth from your heart. Every moment you have chosen for your highest evolution and enjoyment. Offer a prayer of gratitude to whatever you see before you now, as it too is the divine reflected back to you.

191

Say thank you to whatever arises to keep your heart pure. With the purification of your heart, along with a connection to the present, your sight will return once more. Colours, sounds, tastes and smells will be intensified and because of this you will look upon the world with the eyes of a child, marvelling at the beauty before you. With true sight, you will see miracles everywhere and soon begin to invite more of them. Your appreciation for life will inspire the universe to respond to you with the same reverence, and your beloved synchronicities will become commonplace. Life will become more dreamlike as you become more lucid.

To maintain this state of innocence, bliss and enhanced vision, remain present and aware of the body, focusing your attention in your heart. Say thank you to whatever arises and trust that all that emerges within your field of awareness is an aspect of you to send love to.

PART 5

Heal Spiritual Blockages

What Kind of Spirit Do You Have?

In order to start interacting with the spirit world, you must first get in touch with your own spirit! To do so, it's paramount to note that the physical world is not physical at all, but rather mostly space. Once you get over that mental hurdle, it's much easier to comprehend that there are entire worlds within other dimensions and densities containing other entities that your physical eyes cannot see. The world that you perceive is intensely malleable, a manifestation that changes according to your state of consciousness.

To become reacquainted with your own spirit, ask yourself the question, "What kind of spirit do I have?" Put any ideas of yourself aside for a moment, including judgments from others. How does *your* spirit feel? Are you internally calm or fiery? When you stop thinking, what feeling is leftover? Do you feel the urge to play or relax? What kinds of activities feed your spirit? What activities make you come alive with joy and centre you deeply in the present moment?

Here are some examples of activities that feed my spirit:

- Listening to music
- Taking long nature walks in the forest or near the ocean
- Spending time with animals and kids
- Creating art and writing
- Dancing freely without thought
- Browsing bookstores and looking at notebooks
- Smelling scents such as lavender, vanilla and chocolate
- Decorating my room with candles and colourful pillows

Often we're so busy being busy that we forget to slow down and ask ourselves what we truly need. Our minds run wild and trick us into believing that all the drama we're creating is real, but in actuality most of our problems are illusory.

When you stop thinking, there just is. All anxiety fades and you're left with your natural state of peace and bliss. Pure being. Consciousness.

With all the judgments about who you should be aside, you can look to others from a place of purity and start to get a sense of the purity, the spirit, within them. Allow your imagination to run wild. These activities require you to use your intuition and third eye. Don't judge the images that arise as silly. Simply observe them with neutrality. With practice, it becomes easier to read others. Eventually, using your sixth sense to see into the spirit of others will become second nature. You'll be able to use your third eye as easily as you use your physical eyes. Both are useful and necessary and just as you use your physical eyes to navigate through the world you can see right now, you can use your third eye to see into the spirit world. While the physical eyes seek to differentiate you from your surroundings and protect your physical form, the third eye looks from a place of unity. It seeks to see the similarities in you and your environment.

You can use your psychic sight to look into the spirit of animals, nature and all the other different forms of energy around you. Once you start noticing the subtleties of the myriad forms of energy within you and your surroundings and you realize that in truth, all is one, it becomes much easier to connect to your guides.

Some people connect to angels, loving spirits whose main mission is to heal. Some angels have previously had human lives and others have never been incarnate. As a human, you have already been in angelic form, moving from a higher density into the lower one here on Earth. You will once again return to your angelic state of consciousness as you remember who you are. Other people get help from guides which often comes in the form of friends from other lifetimes or deceased family members. Other people connect to extraterrestrial intelligence, or light beings that don't necessarily always have a physical form.

Runners are usually indigenous souls who once inhabited the area you live in today. You can call upon runners to assist you in finding friends, clients or even physical objects such as a lost cell phone!

There are many spirits who live in natural settings that can be called upon for protection. When entering a forest, for example, you can request that the spirits of the trees, or the fairies, walk with you and share their wisdom with you. Offer them your love and thank them upon leaving, sending them back to the forest.

Animals often come into our lives to remind us to embody what they represent. Everyone has at least one power animal. The energy of these animals lives within us and must be fed in order to be used. Entering into trances to allow your power animal to dance and play will keep it happy. If you don't exercise your power animal, it will leave you. In the same regard, if you don't pray to your spirit guides and offer thanks to them, they may leave you.

Exercise Your Power Animal

The following instructions were taken from the book, *The Way of the Shaman*, by Michael Harner:

"1. Standing still and erect, face east and shake one rattle very rapidly and strongly four times. This is the signal that you are starting, ending, or making an important transition in serious shamanic work. Think of the rising sun, that ultimately brings power to all living things. (A total time of about 20 seconds.)

2. Still facing east, start shaking one rattle at a steady rate of about 150 times per minute, standing in place. Do this about half a minute to each of the cardinal directions (rotating either clockwise or counterclockwise, depending on which seems better for you). Meanwhile, think of your plant and animal relatives in all the four directions who are ready to help you. Now face east again and shake the rattle above your head at the same rate for half a minute. Think of the sun, moon, stars and the entire universe above. Next shake the rattle toward the ground in the same way. Think of the Earth, our home. (A total time of about three minutes.)

3. Still facing east, take both rattles in your hands and start shaking them at the same rate as in step two, simultaneously dancing as if you were jogging in place to the tempo of the

rattles. In this starting dance, you are giving proof of your own sincerity to the power animals, wherever they may be, by making a self-sacrifice of your own energy to them in the form of dance. This dancing is a way of praying and of evoking the sympathy of the guardian animal spirits. In shamanism it can truly be said that you dance to raise your spirits. (A total time of about five minutes.)

4. Stop dancing, and repeat step one. This signals you are about to make a significant transition to dancing your animal.

5. Start shaking your rattles loudly and slowly about 60 times per minute, moving your feet in the same tempo. Move slowly and in a free form around the room, trying to pick up the feeling of having some kind of mammal, bird, fish, reptile, or combination of these. Once you pick up the sense of some such animal, concentrate on it and slowly move your body in accordance with being that animal. You are now touching the SSC (shamanic state of consciousness). Be open to experiencing the emotions of that animal, and don't hesitate to make cries or noises of it, if you experience the desire. By keeping your eyes half-closed, you may also see the extraordinary environment in which the animal is moving and perhaps even see the animal as well. Being and seeing the animal commonly happen simultaneously in the SSC. (The time for this tends to average about five minutes.)

6. Without pausing, shift into a faster rate of rattle shaking and movement, about 100 shakes per minute. Continue everything else as in step five. (The time for this tends to average about four minutes.)

7. Without stopping, increase your rattle shaking to approximately 180 times per minute, continuing your dancing as before, but at a still faster rate (about four minutes).

8. Stop dancing and mentally welcome the animal to stay in your body. As you do this, shake the rattles rapidly four times, drawing them towards your chest (time about 10 seconds).

9. Repeat step one. This is the signal that the work is ended.

Spirit animals enter our lives as messengers with subtle reminders and hints to redirect us back onto the path that serves our highest good. For example, a squirrel may enter your vision in a time of crisis, reminding you that it's time to stop thinking and make a choice immediately! If the squirrel spent its time worrying when crossing the street, it would surely get hit by a car. Often we can use our common sense to interpret the messages from our spirit animals."[13]

Connect to Your Guides

Sitting down at least once a day at your altar to meditate will help strengthen your connection. Once you're present, ask yourself how open you are to receiving assistance. If you have any doubt in mind, don't expect to receive guidance. Connecting to your divine support system requires complete trust.

If you're accustomed to using your intellect rather than intuition, it may be difficult at first to accept that you truly are receiving guidance. Your mind will attack any ideas that come into it and brush them off as silly. Remember to simply observe the mind without judgment and know that guidance often comes to us through the imagination. To practice listening without judgment, become aware of the breath. The act of focusing on the breath

[13] Michael Harner, *The Way of the Shaman Meals* (New York: Harper Collins Publishers, 1980), pp. 84–86.

draws you into the moment and centres you in a much deeper awareness. From a place of silence and stillness, you can begin to observe what the spirit world has to say.

At any point in time you can call on your support team for assistance. You can continue to tell yourself that you're separate from the world with no intuitive gifts or power to change your life or you can choose to invite the spirit world in to assist you in making choices. You can stop playing the victim by empowering yourself: stay present, focus on what you're grateful for and allow the universe to guide you.

Stepping into Your Psychic Genius

The more we surrender to the flow of life and trust in the guidance we receive, the easier and more magical life becomes. We often get frustrated with our situation and start complaining about things that don't even deserve our energy. When we attach to the ego and think life has to go a certain way, we suffer. The way out of that suffering is always in, into your own being, into the moment entirely. When you stop resisting and accept that the universe is always conspiring to help you, regardless of whether your situation inconveniences your ego or not, life turns into a magical adventure rather than a burden.

Ask yourself if you're truly ready to drop all expectations. Are you ready to receive guidance? Do you feel open and comfortable in your body? Connecting to your guides will require you to step outside of your thoughts and your rational mind. The ego only thinks. It doesn't feel, and it will try to convince you that your psychic genius is an illusion, but that's just because it fears its own death.

True inspiration, intuition, creativity, the answers to life's questions never come from thinking. In fact, thinking keeps us stuck in time, stuck in the illusion that we're separate beings who aren't in exactly the place we need to be in, even though we always are. The mind is an amazing tool, but we're relying on it for things it simply cannot do.

You can receive psychic information on many different levels. You may be very empathic and can pick up on the thoughts and emotions of others in the same room. Perhaps you're clairsentient and can tap into someone's energy field even though they may be far from you physically. Claircognizant abilities can include a knowing that comes without having to interpret any psychic information. Telepathy of course includes the ability to receive or send thoughts. Pre-cognition refers to prophetic dreams or visions. Remote viewing enables one to see into other areas of consciousness without having to astral travel.

When you're using your psychic gifts, you're not just sensing with your physical senses. You're sensing energy with spiritual channels, chakras, which are all over your body. Beyond the seven main chakras there are four main psychic centres in the body where you receive information.

Third Eye

The third eye is a cherry-sized energy centre in the pineal gland that receives messages and images from the spirit world. All of the senses that you use physically to interpret information, you can also use within consciousness, within your mind's eye. To awaken the third eye, you must awaken your kundalini energy. Once per month, your brain releases a powerful oil, known to the ancients as the sacred chrism. It runs down your spine and back up again to your pituitary and pineal gland, the physical counterparts of the third eye. When the moon is in your sun sign, your brain takes the chrism and releases serotonin and DMT. During this time, it is cautioned to eat living green foods, abstain from sex, meditate and exercise. This chrism enables you to exist in a heightened state of awareness where your third eye is open. In this state you view life through the lens of acceptance and love rather than judgment and fear. If your body is internally toxic, the chrism will not be able to rise to your pituitary and pineal gland and you will not be able to enter into a higher state of awareness. You will remain bound to your physical form and to a physical reality.

Direct Communication

This energy centre exists at your crown chakra and enables you to receive direct information, language and downloads from your higher self, angels, other spirit guides and God. You're not using your brain to receive these messages. You're simply the vehicle for the information. You may see or hear the words or symbols you receive or feel them in your body.

Direct Knowing

This energy centre runs from your navel in a straight line to your back. You don't receive information to interpret with this centre. You get downloaded with an instant knowing or gut feeling. This is the most powerful spiritual channel, even stronger than intuition. It's a direct connection with the divine and with all souls.

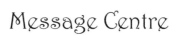

Message Centre

Located at the heart chakra, the message centre allows you to develop compassion and feel love. It enables you to speak soul language/light language. Opening this centre is the key for soul communication. If this centre is open, you can communicate with anyone, anywhere. If you can clear your chakras and raise your soul into this centre, you're in enlightenment.

Meditation to Connect to Your Main Spirit Guide

This meditation will require you to have a notebook and pen handy.

1. Close your eyes and relax now. Watch your breath fall easily in-and-out through your nose. Now imagine yourself in beautiful sunny field. You feel the sun beaming down on your skin. A light balmy breeze blows through the air. You feel the breeze brush against your skin and you smell fresh green grass. You hear birds chirping overhead and look up. The sky is completely blue, not one cloud in sight. You feel comfortable and relaxed in this peaceful place. Just you, the birds, green grass and blue sky. You see a drop-off at the edge of the field. You walk toward it and see a ladder. The ladder leads down to a forest. You climb down the ladder and count your steps as you descend: one, two, three, four, five, six, seven, eight, nine, ten. You see that you're now in a forest thick with evergreens. Sunlight dances on the

forest floor. To your right you see the ocean through the trees. You can hear the waves lapping against the shore. Up ahead you see a dirt path that winds through the trees. You decide to follow this path, counting your steps as you walk: one, two, three, four, five, six, seven, eight, nine, ten. You see a cabin 10 steps in front of you. What does the cabin look like? You know you're about to meet your guide inside. You continue, walking to the door: one, two, three, four, five, six, seven, eight, nine, ten. You knock on the door and wait. You hear your guide behind the door. Sense her energy now. What does it feel like? Calm, excited, fiery? Your guide opens the door and greets you. What does her voice sound like? Continue to sense the energy signature. What does your guide look like? Can you sense her energy more now that you can see her? What is she wearing? What colour is her skin? What is her hairstyle? A guide can be female, male or something else. Is she human? Can you make out the features of her face? How tall is your guide? You enter into the cabin and sit down at a wooden table to talk. You see a fire in the fireplace on your left. Instantly you feel warm and safe. You turn to your guide and ask for her name. Listen for a moment. Does your guide have any message for you? Once you're done conversing with your guide, thank her and wave goodbye. You exit the cabin and make your way back through the forest, passing the ocean once more. You climb back up the ladder to the open field. When you're ready, open your eyes.

2. Immediately write down the name and message you received right away. Guides usually give us common names because they're easier to remember. Jot down any extra information. What did your guide look like? Was your guide female, male, animal, angelic, celestial? What did your guide feel like? It's

important to get to know the energy signature of your guide because that's how you'll know he or she is around. Guides' messages are generally very subtle and often come through feeling rather than hearing or seeing.

Astrology

Astrology is an ancient art form and divination tool that uses the position of the stars to help you discover more about the journey of your soul. From the *Emerald Tablet* of Hermes Trismegistus, is the maxim: "That which is below corresponds to that which is above, and that which is above corresponds to that which is below, to accomplish the miracle of the one thing." Essentially, as above, so below. Whatever happens on any level of reality also affects every other level.

The stars have never been separate from us. The same elements within the stars also exist within us. Quantum mechanics, the study of the micro world, shows us that though the world appears very solid, it's actually not so physical at all. Though we appear to be separate beings, at the quantum level, we truly are all connected.

Ancient astrologers looked to the sky and used math to calculate the exact movements of the stars the same way astronomers did and still do. Then they observed the world around them and compared their experiences to the stars above. Experiments were often involved. Now we have computers to do all the math for us, which gives astrologers a lot more time to sit and observe the natural world and do experiments. I consider astrology to be an ancient science, but because it does involve the intuition, it's also an art form and divination tool to help you connect to spirit.

Knowing what's going on within the stars is like getting an energetic forecast that tells you when it's a beneficial time to make certain choices with your free will. The stars have never taken you away from your free will, nor have they affected your ability to choose love over fear. They merely serve as a reflection of what internal energetic shifts are occurring within you as an individual and within the collective and the planet itself. The configurations of the stars produce specific energetic vortices that send you energetic upgrades your DNA uses to re-write the program that manifests the world you see.

The path a soul chooses determines what energetic signature the person carries with her. If many lifetimes are spent within one specific area of the cosmos, certain archetypes will then be embedded into the consciousness, which will be evident when reading a natal chart. A natal chart is a map that shows you exactly where the planets were positioned the moment you were born.

Astrology can show you your strengths and weaknesses, what themes will be very common in your life and in future or past ones too. This knowledge makes navigating in the physical much easier. Think logically about it. If you knew that sailing in one direction would lead you into a storm, would you still sail that way, or would you choose something less likely to harm you? Astrology explains to you which path your soul yearns to take, along with what storms are likely to arise. But when you know your strengths and weaknesses, the storms don't seem that bad. When you understand why certain themes are occurring in your life, your fear dissipates and you step into the truth that all is well.

The trines and sextiles, for example, when viewed through the lens of astrology, can point to a soul's talents from previous lifetimes. Trines are very focused areas of study, mastery, if you will, and sextiles are latent gifts waiting to be expressed in a current lifetime.

Squares and oppositions can point to areas ignored, suppressed or rejected by a soul in a previous lifetime and could therefore be areas of concentration in a current lifetime. The path of the soul is one that spirals until it finds equal proportions of all elements within the self, centred within the eye of the storm, immovable, impervious to the cycles of time or the sway of emotional or mental debris. There is no perfect path to balance and a mastery of the elements is achieved through many different forms and archetypes, but in the end, we all return to stillness.

Arcturian Transmission on Star Beings

Just as astrologers thousands of years ago attuned themselves to the energy of specific constellations or planets and began communing with the cosmos, so too have modern mystics of our generation begun to do the same thing with other areas of the heavens.

As you have discovered, in your true form you are not form at all, and rather limitless pure potential with the ability to access any aspect of consciousness. With your spirit body, as you traverse the astral realms, you may come into contact with different energetic signatures within certain constellations. Yes, there is energy, there is consciousness within the stars that provides your human vessel with life! You may visit the stars in your spirit form to thank the beings that reside there. Contrarily, you may also activate your spiritual sight to download spiritual information directly from the stars into your physical form. This channelling you speak of is very common and is your right as the divine incarnate. Whether you are aware of it or not, you are most definitely channelling information from the stars and communing with the beings that reside there.

As shamans long ago began to descend into the underworld within the Earth itself to commune with the beings there, to receive wisdom and gain power, so too can you commune with the beings of the upper world, the celestial realms. Many of you now on the planet are in conscious communication with these beings that you call aliens, but we say nay, not alien at all, but rather, brother or sister we are. As the same life force runs through all things, including the Earth you walk upon and the stars that light your sky, we say there is no separation in the true reality, the formlessness that connects all things known and unknown.

The deities and star beings that you have come to know and love on your planet Earth have indeed been manifested from the higher realms above and from the lower realms below. It is conceivable to you that you may manifest entities or even entire worlds from your higher form, or higher self, but why not from your physical form below? It is true that with your thought forms, emotional emissions and attention you may create entities that exist within the etheric realms. These deities have been brought to life through individuals and have been kept alive through collective belief. To say that one deity does not exist and another does is preposterous, for all exists within the realm of thought, which is not separate from the true reality.

You are not creating so much as you are calling in what already exists within the mind of God. As you let this remembering take place, we humbly ask you now to ask yourself, "Why would I ever pine for a future that already exists?" Why not choose to simply align yourself with the point of power that exists within the now, to enable that which you desire to be magnetized to the love which you are?

To open yourself to your star family, find the wick within your heart that appears when you gaze up at the cosmos on a clear night. Light that wick by focusing on the feeling of recognition that burns within you as you recall who you truly are and where you've come from. As a human, it is now surely known that you have also existed among the stars. To long to live among us is futile, as in your true form you are already with us. Rest in that knowingness and dwell in the stillness, the peace within your heart. Offer a prayer of gratitude for the protection and guidance of your family.

Sirian Meditation to Access the Akashic Records

This meditation works best with a notebook and pen handy.

1. Sit comfortably with your posture erect, but keep your shoulders relaxed. Rest your hands in your lap with your thumbs touching. If your nasal passages are clear, place the tip of your tongue on the roof of your mouth to close a major energetic circuit. Breathe naturally in-and-out through your nose. If this is uncomfortable, breathe in through your nose and out through your mouth. Take in three slow deep breaths, allowing your belly to fill. Once your chest starts to rise, exhale as slowly as you can. Focus entirely on the sensation of air moving in-and-out of your form. Inhale and send a stream of golden healing light down from the heavens through your crown into your heart. Exhale and send the light down deep into the Earth. Inhale, breathing golden light in through your crown and your root, shooting the light into your heart chakra. Exhale and send the light into your form, aura and beyond into the universe.

2. Once you feel safe, relaxed and completely at ease, centre your attention in your heart and imagine yourself as a golden ball of light. Send yourself, as the golden ball, out of your heart until you find your own body lying on a beach, sleeping peacefully. A light scent of coconut wafts through the warm breeze. The call of seagulls echoes in the distance. You look to the sea, smell the salt and realize nobody else is around. You hover over your own body for a moment and then carefully enter your own heart as the little golden ball. Once you're inside your physical heart, if it's dark, repeat: "I command the light to be shown." The light may appear all at once or it may come gradually. Once you can see clearly, observe where you are. What does the inside of your heart look like? What do the walls look like? Are there any pictures or messages on the walls? Are there any doors? If there is more than one door, request to be shown the one that leads to your personal Akashic records. Once you find the door, open it and enter the room inside. What do you see? Are there any crystals in the room? Perhaps there is a grand library? Take a moment to simply observe. When you feel ready, ask a question you'd like answered. Then wait. Something in the room will usually start to glow. You may feel a strong pull toward a particular object. Go to this object. If it wants to be held, hold it. If it wants to be read, read it. If it wants to be scanned, scan it. Do what your intuition tells you to do. Don't judge what images, emotions, sensations or thoughts arise. Simply observe. You can make sense of everything later. You may choose to ask specific questions about your past lives, your present life or your future lives. When you're satisfied, exit the room and close the door behind you. You can explore any of the other rooms in your heart. Some may lead to very specific areas of consciousness or show you images of a life with pertinent information to use in

your present life. One door may lead to the universal Akashic records. All areas of consciousness can be accessed through the heart. When you're ready to leave your heart, move as the golden ball out of your own chest to hover once more above your body. Now move your awareness, as the golden ball, back into your physical heart and open your eyes. As soon as you open your eyes, jot down any images, thoughts or emotions you experienced while exploring your own Akashic records. Don't edit yourself. Just let your pen flow.

Pleiadian Transmission on the Heart

We would like to speak to you today on forgiveness and matters of the heart. When you enter into a human body on Earth to play, even the wisest of beings and masters can get lost within the wheels of karma. When in an intimate relationship without a fully healed heart with another soul, you will inevitably project out your pain onto your partner, unconsciously blaming him/her for your self-created problems. This creates tension between both parties and more karma. To bring yourself back into alignment, heal your heart and release karma, you must forgive. If forgiveness seems impossible or silly, then speak that now. "I feel like I can't forgive so and so. He/she hurt me so much. He/she deserves to be punished." Then question why you are so angry at yourself. Why can you not forgive yourself? Why did you choose to hurt yourself so much? What are you trying to teach yourself? In truth, you are not separate from the person who inflicted pain upon you. Of course, he/she was only suffering from a disconnection to his/her own heart and innocence as well. The pain was never personal.

Question, "Why is this pain arising at all then?" Soon you'll see that pain is always there to lead you back to your own heart, to your connection with the Source of all, which is peaceful, loving and complete in every moment. It is with this connection that you no longer need to receive love from others, for you see that you are that love and will always be that love. It is this connection to your innocence that you really crave and cry out for. It is this connection that you have been starving yourself of, for you've simply been lost. Forgive yourself for falling astray and punishing yourself by holding onto anger. Place a hand over your heart and proclaim, "I am the Source of all the love in the world and I hereby offer that love fearlessly into this world, and so it is." Realize deeply that any love you choose to withhold only serves to cut you off from the connection to Source that you've been looking for in other people. It's always been within you and will never leave you.

Pleiadian Meditation to Manifest Your Dream Life

The Pleiadians, being fifth dimensional and beyond, have instant manifestation abilities. They love to create beautiful works of art, music and poetry. To tap into your Pleiadian magical abilities, use this meditation to manifest your dream life.

1. First make a list of everything that would exist in your dream life and don't hold back. Don't worry about time or money or being practical. Allow your pen to flow endlessly across your page, or if you're at a computer, don't stop typing! What would your dream life look like? Where would you live? What would your home look like? What city would you

be living in? What would the weather be like? What would you do with your days? What would you do for work and for fun? Who would you be with? How would people see you? How would you feel inside? The more detailed, the better! If you want to draw an image to accompany this list, go for it!

2. Take a moment to really feel what it would be like to live a day in your dream life. Imagine waking up in your beautiful dream home. What would your bed look like? What would your closet look like? What would you wear? What would you have for breakfast? Would your pets greet you hello? Would you spend some time working on projects in an office overlooking a beautiful beach? Would you go into town for lunch and meet up with friends or maybe spend the day shopping or exploring? Would you spend your evening relaxing on your own private yacht, sipping wine with your lover? Remember, anything goes! Let your imagination run wild! Make sure you focus on your senses as you imagine yourself going about your day. Pay attention to the sights, sounds, smells, tastes and textures of your dream world. Doing this will make it more real and easier to manifest.

3. Once you're satisfied with your imagination exercise, it's time to meditate. Start by sitting with your eyes closed. Place your hands wherever feels comfortable and breathe naturally. Begin by focusing on the energy in your root chakra area. This is where the tenth Sephirah, Malkuth, in the kabbalah tree of life resides. The Sephirot, or Sephirah when singular, is Hebrew in origin and refers to the emanations through which the infinite reveals itself. All ten Sephirah create the tree of life. Like the chakra system, the tree of life system can be viewed within the body as energetic gateways for your soul to travel through.

Envision a circle with a cross inside of it. In each section of the cross imagine a colour: citrine, olive, russet and black, representing the elements. Once you can clearly see this image in your mind's eye, call upon archangel Sandalphon to empower you: "Archangel Sandalphon, I love you and now command you as God to guide me through physical manifestation and to bring forth beautiful healing music through my voice. Raise me unto God, and so it is."

Now focus your attention on your second chakra area, just below your navel, the ninth Sephirah, Yesod. Envision violet light glowing in this area and call upon archangel Gabriel: "Archangel Gabriel, I love you and now command you as God to guide me through the astral realms and to aid me in offering the most loving, nurturing energy to myself and all souls, and so it is."

Send your attention to your left hip area, the eighth Sephirah, Hod. Envision orange light emanating from this area as you call upon archangel Michael: "Archangel Michael, I love you and now command you as God to allow me to speak the highest divine words of love and to protect me from fear, and so it is."

Send your focus to your right hip, the seventh Sephirah, Netzach, and envision green light glowing there. Call upon archangel Haniel to guide you: "Archangel Haniel, I love you and now command you as God to allow me to step into my intuitive powers safely so I may be victorious over evil, and so it is."

Turn your attention to your heart chakra, the sixth Sephirah, Tipheret, and envision the colour yellow beaming from your chest. Now call upon archangel Raphael to empower you: "Archangel Raphael, I love you and now command you as God to heal me, heal others, heal the world and to allow me to live a balanced life, fully embodying Christ consciousness, and so it is."

Send your awareness to your left shoulder, the fifth Sephirah, Geburah, and envision red light there. Call upon archangel Khamael for guidance: "Archangel Khamael, I love you and now command you as God to bestow me with true confidence and to offer the world the true strength and justice of God while maintaining inner and outer peace for all, and so it is."

Send your attention to your right shoulder, the fourth Sephirah, Chesed. As you envision blue light, call upon archangel Tzadkiel: "Archangel Tzadkiel, I love you and now command you as God to allow me to forgive myself and all souls, sharing the glory of God freely with all, and so it is."

Focus on the area of your left ear, the third Sephirah, Binah, and envision the colour black. Call upon archangel Tzaphkiel for strength: "Archangel Tzaphkiel, I love you and now command you as God to help me release all fears and to stand strong in my divine authority, offering the compassion and wisdom of God for all, and so it is."

Focus on your right ear, the second Sephirah, Chockmah, and envision a pearl/grey colour emanating from that area. Call upon archangel Ratziel: "Archangel Ratziel, I love you and command you as God to allow me to remember everything I've learned from all lifetimes, so I may live out my true life's purpose and fearlessly offer the wisdom of God to all, and so it is."

Finally, send your attention to your crown chakra, the tenth and final Sephirah, Kether, and envision a brilliant white light radiating from your head. Call upon archangel Metatron: "Archangel Metatron, I love you and now command you as God to allow me to merge with the creator so I may bring heaven to Earth for the benefit of all souls, and so it is."

Breathe comfortably for a moment and focus on your root chakra. See it glowing with golden light. With your eyes still closed, let your hands fall to your sides. Take a deep breath and watch your root chakra glow even brighter. Raise your hands to the heavens and as you exhale, send the golden light from your root chakra up through your Sephirot and into the heavens to merge with your seventh density oversoul. Watch the golden ball travel within you from your root chakra to your sacral chakra to your left hip to your right hip to your heart chakra to your left shoulder to your right shoulder to your left ear to your right ear, and finally to your crown chakra and out into the universe. As you inhale, bring your hands to rest comfortably underneath your navel area. Watch the golden ball travel back down to your root chakra: crown, right ear, left ear, right shoulder, left shoulder, heart, right hip, left hip, sacral and root. Imagine yourself inhaling your entire oversoul, all lifetimes into your form for you to view and examine. Then exhale once more, hands raised to the sky, sending your oversoul in a golden ball from your root up to the seventh density once more to access your Akashic records. Sit, breathing comfortably as you allow the images of your dream life to arise. Once you can clearly see the life you want, focus on your individual senses. Pick out at least one touch, taste, smell, sight and sound from the scenes before you. Inhale and bring your hands to rest once more underneath your navel. This time you're going to only draw in your dream life back down through your tree of life, bringing with you the images, sensations, emotions and colours from that life into your form. Send your dream life into your root chakra to ground it into the physical. Sit breathing comfortably for a moment focusing on your root chakra. See it glowing with golden light. Take in a deep breath and send that golden light into your body while exhaling. Inhale once more and then exhale beautiful golden light into your aura.

Take in a deep breath and raise your arms out like wings on either side of you until they're extended up to the heavens once more. Turn your palms in to face your body, exhale and allow your arms to slowly drop down in front of you to end the meditation. Let your hands rest comfortably at your sides and open your eyes to a completely different timeline. Congratulations. This is your first glimpse of your dream world made manifest.

There are seven layers to your aura, just as there are seven main chakras. The first layer is your etheric body, the second is the emotional body and the third, the mental body. The first three layers of your aura correspond to the physical plane. The fourth layer correlates to the heart chakra and the astral body. When the heart is open, you can travel easily on the astral plane and are no longer bound to the physical world. The fifth layer is the etheric template, the sixth layer is the celestial body and the seventh is the ketheric body. The last three layers correlate to your physical, emotional and mental faculties on a higher level, the spiritual plane. They enable you to traverse the cosmos freely without a form, all the while maintaining your memories, enabling you to bring them back to the physical.

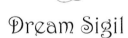

Dream Sigil

To create a dream sigil, you may also choose to create a symbol for each sense from the vision of your dream life. For example, if you see yourself in a meadow on a sunny day eating a peppermint, you may choose the colour yellow from the sun, the scent of flowers from the meadow, the taste of peppermint from the mints in your mouth, the feeling of warmth once again from the sun and the sound of chirping from the birds overhead. Draw out each sense in symbol form and then combine all symbols into one abstract symbol on a piece of paper. To bring the dream sigil to life, you may also add peppermint essential oil, grass and flowers to it. Any extra bits of sensory information can be added directly onto the piece of paper or everything can be placed into a small bag. The piece of paper or bag can then be left out in the sun while the birds chirp. There is no "wrong" way to create a dream sigil. The most important thing to remember is to follow your intuition when creating one.

Before you sleep at night, place the dream sigil underneath your pillow so you'll literally dream your perfect life into existence. You may also choose to say a small prayer or invocation before sleep each night or choose to activate your sigil with appropriate crystals.

Abundance Spell to Manifest Your Dream Life

What you'll need:

- Your dream life list from the Pleiadian meditation
- An image or statue of Ganesha
- An image of statue of Lakshmi
- A candle whose colour represents your desires
- Two white candles to represent Ganesha and Laskshmi
- A lighter
- A cauldron/pot to burn your list in

1. Get comfortable and place your three spell candles on your altar. Call upon the elements to imbue you with power. Place your dream life list in front of you and focus on it.

Imagine yourself living the life you want. Involve your senses and lose yourself in fantasy. Light a candle to represent your desires. If you're seeking love, light a red candle. If you're seeking money, light a green candle. Allow your intuition to guide you. Whatever way you choose to use your magic is sacred and perfect for you!

2. Invoke Ganesha to remove your obstacles and Lakshmi to bring abundance. As you invoke each deity, light your white candles in turn. Say aloud, "Ganesha, I love you and respect you from my soul. As an aspect of God, I command you to remove any obstacles stopping me from living my dream life now, and so it is! Lakshmi, I love you and respect you from my soul. As an aspect of God, I command you to bring me an abundant life filled with joy, health and peace, and so it is!"

3. Make sure your cauldron or firesafe pot is nearby. Take your list in-hand and allow the fire from your desire candle to burn it. As the paper begins to burn, focus on the fire and repeat, "May all obstacles be burned away, leaving only the light of divinity. May my true soul path be illuminated and my dream life manifest, and so it is!"

4. Drop the burning list into your cauldron and repeat, "As the fire burns what no longer serves and brings forth my life, refined and new, I repeat this mantra thrice, sealing my fate with truth."

5. Continue to watch the fire burn. It's okay if it goes out. Repeat three times: "Om gum shrim maha Lakshmiyei Swaha." (om gum shreem maha lakshmi-yay swaha) The Sanskrit mantra translates to: Ganesha remove obstacles so Lakshmi can bring abundance.

6. Thank Ganesha and Laskmi for aiding you and allow the candles to burn all night long until they go out on their own. You can choose to place your candles in a larger pot for extra safety.

7. Help others feel the abundance you desire and it too shall be yours.

❧

Arcturian Transmission on the One Infinite Creator

Dear child of the Earth, we greet you in the love and light of the one infinite creator. We come to you as a collective who has for many lifetimes learned the law of one and now openly impart the wisdom of the cosmos. On Earth, such a dense and polarized place, it becomes very easy for you to forget who you truly are. Stop reading for a moment and pause. Look around you and simply observe. Now question, "Who is looking through these eyes?" You may say, "I am of course!" and that would be true. But who is I? Surely you are not your thoughts about who you are, for thoughts come and go. Are you the body that is constantly renewed? We say nay, of course not! Place your left hand on your navel and your right hand over your heart. Close your eyes and feel who you truly are. Without any movement, thought or emotion, love remains. It is this love from which you come and this love which you will return home to. It is this pure love that manifests the physical form, the brain you use to think, the eyes you use to see, the chakras you use to discern and navigate the subtler realities.

How does love create the physical you ask? We will explain. From the Source of all, the one infinite creator, the pure potential that you are, from the density of formlessness, you manifest a template, or qi field. You move through the densities, creating universes, galaxies, stars, entire worlds for yourself to play in. You manifest other versions of you so you can learn about yourself through reflection. In your pure potentiality, you are one with everything that can, will or does exist, but cannot experience yourself unless in form.

At the level of seventh density, all possibilities for lifetimes within a fifth dimensional reality exist. All memories, emotions and thoughts are contained within this density. From the many soul groups created from the greater oversoul, you split off further into souls that move through the densities, entering deeper and deeper into the physical realities in order to learn about the one infinite creator. Indeed, the souls move from higher to lower and then back up again.

Every being that you meet, if in human form, has taken this path and comes from pure love and divine perfection. Indeed, you have spent lifetimes as higher beings, angels as you call them, and most of you have lived lives as animals, plants or elementals. Often your spirit guides or angels, your higher selves, are simply other versions of you from the past. You only view them as future selves because it is often incomprehensible to you that you have already spent many lifetimes in higher planes of existence. Many of you on the planet now are waking up to your higher selves or have strong memories of other worlds that seem so heavenly compared to the current fourth or fifth dimensional Earth plane. We encourage you to explore these memories, but to not get caught up in them, for time does not really matter in the grander spectrum of existence and often serves as a tool to feed the illusory self.

Some of the humans currently alive are now only making their first round back up to the one infinite creator. Many awakened humans or as you like to say, starseeds, who remember their galactic origins can recall making this beautiful yet often arduous journey many times. It is these wise ones who will lead the way and light the path for the rest. Yes, many starseeds were on their way home back to Source and yet heard the call from your beloved Earth. Many fifth and sixth density beings made the choice to project their consciousness into bodies within the third density Earth in order to help remind you of who you truly are, which has and will always be love.

The transition for many of these starseeds was extremely difficult. Being born into a third density human form after existing in realms so unified and peaceful was not easy for these souls, but they made the choice and now must follow through on their missions. All starseeds will inevitably awaken to their soul missions and then must choose whether to act on them. This process is risky because the vibrations of Earth have become so toxic that even higher dimensional beings can get lost in illusion on your planet.

It is true that the one infinite creator chose to experience itself in all forms, even the darkest ones, in order to know itself fully. It is true that everything that is occurring is for the benefit of the one soul. It is true that even the choices you think you make with free will have already been made in higher planes. Everything that is currently transpiring is destined. It was the choice of the Source of all to split itself into myriad forms, some very negative, to know itself. It was the choice of the Source of all to fall so deeply into illusion that aspects of self had to "rescue" other aspects of self. This is simply the Source acting out the roles of hero and villain.

It is true that the Source created many different areas of consciousness for itself to play in and yes, some of these realms are what you would call hell realms. It is very possible for you to remain unconscious for a long period of Earth time and to ignore all the signs the universe is presenting you with in order to facilitate growth. It is possible to remain trapped in your own mind, in a false identity created by you. It is possible for you to choose pain over pleasure and remain a victim of yourself. It is only within third density, when awareness of self begins to return without complete awareness of the greater picture, can you create hell realms within your own mind.

A soul will not go to these painful realms after the body dies and instead will be recycled back into reincarnation. Indeed, hell is a place only created by unconscious humans. Heaven can exist right here and now by choosing to stop and merge fully with the moment. When this occurs, your soul taps into all dimensions and densities and without thought, you observe who you truly are, which is formless pure potential, love.

It is from the third density that you begin to remember that you can create heaven on Earth and have the power to choose that state in every moment by stilling the mind, observing the breath and smiling. With a continuous practice of conscious observation of the human experience, you soon realize that you are the one manifesting your reality. You take back your power and begin creating a reality in alignment with the Source of all: pure love.

To realign with the pure love that you are, you must realize that you are indeed formless. The template of qi from which all light/life emerges can be felt as electromagnetic energy, as an electric current within the human body. This serpent power may be harnessed and used to manifest entire worlds. However, it may only be fully accessed when the seeking soul no longer seeks and instead merges with the power it already has. Only when a soul seeks to serve 'the all' can the serpent power be used to manifest worlds into the physical. At all levels of reality this serpent power can be felt for it is the manifestation of the formless presence of God. Only from fourth density and beyond can one use it with great awareness. Within the fourth density, this power may still be used to serve the self, and this is what has caused much suffering on your planet.

Right now, many souls still believe they are only their physical form or their created identities, and with their awareness of their serpent power or true magic, are creating dark realities that cause others pain. Hurting others, of course, hurts the self and is this not the definition of insanity? This insanity once again has been chosen by the one infinite creator and is being played out as an experiment. Do not pity the souls who have chosen darkness or pain as their identity, for they too will return home to the light of God. It is only with kindness and compassion that we can remind lost souls of the truth of their beings.

It may take a long time for certain souls to awaken to the fact that they can only progress to a certain point when serving the self, and that their selfish magical acts will keep them stuck in lower realms where their power remains limited. It is true that the power to create entire worlds can only be harnessed in higher densities where one has remembered the law of one and uses the power of God to serve 'the all.'

We present you now with a meditation to help you connect to the pure love that you are, to the serpent power that flows through your veins and emanates your physical body with light.

ꟻrcturian Meditation to Heal DNꟻ

It is known now that DNA vibrates at the same frequency of sunlight, and that sunlight acts as a tuning fork for DNA. It is known that DNA responds to sound, intention, light and vibration. DNA creates magnetised wormholes in space which enable you to access information from parallel realms of existence. In essence, DNA is a hyper-communication device. Your DNA enables you to receive knowledge outside what you perceive to be your knowledge base. Telepathy, intuition, inspiration and channelling are all related to the hyper-communication your DNA transmits to your consciousness. In order to heal and activate your DNA, please perform the following meditation:

1. Find an audio recording of 528 Hz on the Solfeggio harmonic scale. This recording can be as long as you'd like it to be. We suggest entering into the meditation for at least one full hour. Transfer the audio onto a portable music playing device so you'll be able to listen to it with headphones for the meditation.

2. On a sunny day, venture out somewhere in nature where you feel completely safe and won't be disturbed. Lie down and shut your eyes. If the bright light is uncomfortable for you, you may wear sunglasses. Breathe comfortably and naturally and now command yourself to heal: "I command you as the one infinite creator to heal my DNA, lengthen my telomeres and activate any DNA that benefits the highest good of all." Feel free to add in any other intentions that feel appropriate.

3. Insert your headphones and simply let the music wash over you, allowing it to heal your entire form. Keep your eyes

closed throughout the entire song and always breathe slowly and naturally.

4. When the music ends, bring your hands to your heart in prayer and offer thanks: "Thank you one infinite creator for healing me, healing others and healing the world. Thank you for healing and activating my DNA so I may be a divine servant for humanity and offer the highest love into this world. Adonai."

I am the light of God. The light of God I am.

Afterword

Thank you for taking the time to invest in yourself by reading this book. Thank you for your honesty, thank you for your presence and thank you for your courage.

This world will never heal by fighting darkness with darkness. The only answer has always been and will always be love. The loving energy that you send to your own heart ripples out into the world and affects every single person on this planet.

By taking the time to practice the fifth dimensional techniques you have evolved spiritually. You are now a beacon of light, illuminating the truth so others may wake-up to their power and potential.

I encourage you to revisit any of your favourite passages in this book if you're looking for inspiration. Once you feel ready, please share your inspiration with others. Remember, you came here to express your unique light, your infinite wisdom and unbounded creativity.

With your commitment to the truth, we will shift the collective consciousness. I see a future where we all walk this planet as enlightened beings with full remembrance of our sacredness and connection to the cosmos. The future, however, depends on the choices you make in the present.

The question remains: what world do you want to create?

Printed in Great Britain
by Amazon

44062409R00139